CU00793448

Trauma fragments our ability to think and ma
to overcome the fragmentation by long winde
that we can no more carry than run with a bro
Turnage offers with brilliant simplicity and wi:
chase and grounds me in what I know to be tr
offer you hope without denying the depths of
be with Jesus.
DAN AND BECKY ALLENDER
FOUNDERS OF THE ALLENDER CENTER FOR TRAUMA AND ABUSE, AND FOUNDING PRESIDENT OF THE SEATTLE SCHOOL
FOR THEOLOGY AND PSYCHOLOGY

To recover is to return to normal. But what is normal? Because our lives are bruised
and broken by the Fall we know deep down, that is an unrealistic target. Elizabeth
Turnage yet again invites fellow sufferers to be nourished daily by doses of life-giving
gospel truths. She encourages her readers to set their sights beyond a temporal cure
or easy solution—Christ-likeness.
KAREN HODGE
COORDINATOR OF WOMEN'S MINISTRIES FOR THE PRESBYTERIAN CHURCH IN AMERICA (PCA)
AUTHOR OF *TRANSFORMED: LIFE-TAKER TO LIFE-GIVER AND LIFE-GIVING LEADERSHIP*

When the storms of life crash into our lives, the devastation left behind is often
overwhelming. Recovery and healing is slow and arduous. Elizabeth Turnage's
devotional is for all those laboring toward recovery. *From Recovery to Restoration* is a
hope-filled, gospel-laced, and Christ-exalting book which invites us into God's story
of redemption and helps us see how he is at work to redeem and restore all things,
even the aftermath of our personal losses, heartaches, and trials.
CHRISTINA FOX
WRITER, COUNSELOR, SPEAKER
AUTHOR OF *A HEART SET FREE: A JOURNEY TO HOPE THROUGH THE PSALMS OF LAMENT*

Having personally known real crisis, both surviving Hurricane Katrina and Stage
four colon cancer, I found that Elizabeth Turnage's thoughtful book perfectly cap-
tures the landscape of loss after devastating personal events, as she guides the reader
through these difficult times to courage, peace, hope and the eventual restoration of
all things.
JAMIE ATEN
EXECUTIVE DIRECTOR, HUMANITARIAN DISASTER INSTITUTE
AUTHOR OF *A WALKING DISASTER*

Whether it be in the midst of physical pain, addiction, abandonment, abuse, or habitual sin, Elizabeth will redirect your gaze over and over through Scripture to meditate not on the gaping hole of your loss, but on the relentless pursuit of Jesus's love. *From Recovery to Restoration* is full of encouragement, practical steps, and reminders of the truth of God's faithfulness where trauma and tragedy have dominated. If pain has seemingly stolen some or all of your hope in the gospel, this is the book for you.

HOPE BLANTON AND CHRISTINE GORDON
AUTHORS, AT HIS FEET STUDIES

What are you recovering from? A life-threatening illness or injury? The loss of a loved one? A financial setback? Abandonment? Life seems out of control? Uncertainty reigns?

Elizabeth Turnage's book *From Recovery to Restoration* was written for such a time as this. Sharing from her personal experiences of pain and loss, Elizabeth writes vulnerably and with vivid word pictures. In this 60-day devotional, covering myriad causes of trauma, you will journey through Scripture for encouragement and hope, connecting with the likes of King David in a dark valley, assured that the Good Shepherd was always with him. Each chapter guides you to personal prayer and reflection. Recovery is possible and restoration becomes reality.

JUDY DOUGLASS
WRITER, SPEAKER, ENCOURAGER
AUTHOR OF *WHEN YOU LOVE A PRODIGAL*, OFFICE OF THE PRESIDENT, CRU

Leading a mission agency, you see first-hand what it looks like for things to break down and fall apart. From personal losses, to physical danger, to the heartbreaking grief of ministry in a broken world, every cross-cultural worker faces hardship and crisis as a normal part of their calling. In honest, direct language, *From Recovery to Restoration* helps all who are suffering loss recalibrate their hearts and refocus their eyes on Jesus, who is our only true source of hope. The gospel not only gives us the freedom to name our need, our brokenness and our suffering—it also leads us back to the One who is making all things new, including our hearts. I'm profoundly grateful for the way Elizabeth Turnage models that journey for us.

BOB OSBORNE
EXECUTIVE DIRECTOR, SERGE

It's always inspiring to see women like Elizabeth not only survive adversity but find purpose and promise along the way. Her light shines brightly in her newest book that is full of thoughtful meditations and profound invitations that encourage us to encounter Jesus and keep the faith despite our pain.

DANIELLE RIPLEY-BURGESS
TWO-TIME COLON CANCER SURVIVOR AND AUTHOR OF *BLUSH: HOW I BARELY SURVIVED 17*

After the death of our son Mark, I would have soaked in Elizabeth Turnage's book, *From Recovery to Restoration*. Elizabeth comes alongside broken people as a dear friend would, whispering in our ears, "This is the way, walk in it." Scripture that not only comforts but instructs a wounded person fills the pages and helps hurting people move from the waiting room to recovery and finally to restoration. Invite Elizabeth to walk with you in your journey toward restoration.

SHARON W. BETTERS
DIRECTOR OF RESOURCE DEVELOPMENT
MARKINC MINISTRIES

With rich theological insight and refreshing transparency, Elizabeth Turnage helps us understand our lives as part of God's story of redemption and renewal. Day by day, the reader is invited into the unfolding mystery of God's providence and encouraged to remember that the God who laughs and sings is also the God who suffered and died to make us whole again. This book is a gift to the church.

JOEL TREICK
SENIOR PASTOR, PINEWOODS PRESBYTERIAN CHURCH

Recovery rooms bring us face to face with the brokenness, hurt and difficulty of our present life. Knocking us off our planned course, those sterile rooms can be some of the hardest places to remember our source of hope. I encourage you to invite Elizabeth to sit with you there. She does not give oversimplified answers, but instead points us to Jesus, the One who has the words of eternal life. As one who has been there before, she engages the questions deeply and searches the Scriptures with as much intensity and clarity, making her a comforting companion for those longing for such fellowship.

MEAGHAN MAY
REGIONAL ADVISOR FOR WOMEN'S MINISTRIES NORTHEAST
PRESBYTERIAN CHURCH IN AMERICA (PCA)

In each of these meditations, Elizabeth tenderly reminds us that we are not victims in our pain or difficult circumstances. She gently reminds us that God is present with us in the hard spaces of our lives, and his presence gives us great hope. Each meditation lifts our eyes to see beyond our present reality to a future glory. What a wonderful resource for anyone who longs for restoration!

ABBY HUTTO, DIRECTOR OF SPIRITUAL FORMATION, STORY PRESBYTERIAN CHURCH, WESTERVILLE, OHIO
AUTHOR, *GOD FOR US: DISCOVERING THE HEART OF THE FATHER THROUGH THE LIFE OF THE SON*

FOREWORD BY SCOTTY SMITH

FROM

RECOVERY

TO

RESTORATION

60 MEDITATIONS FOR
FINDING PEACE & HOPE
IN CRISIS

Elizabeth Reynolds Turnage

Living Story
www.elizabethturnage.com
etlivingstory@gmail.com

Volume discounts are available. Please contact the publisher at etlivingstory@gmail.com for information.
Cover and interior design: Erik M. Peterson
Page composition: Charity Walton with Good Shepherd Publications

ISBN: 978-0-9980321-3-9 (print)
ISBN: 978-0-9980321-4-6 (ebook)
Publisher's Cataloging-in-Publication Data

Names: Turnage, Elizabeth Reynolds, author. | Smith, Scotty, 1950-, foreword author.

Title: From Recovery to Restoration : 60 meditations for finding peace and hope in crisis / Elizabeth Reynolds Turnage ; foreword by Scotty Smith.

Series: Peace & Hope in Crisis

Description: Includes bibliographical references and index. | Pensacola, FL: Living Story, 2020.

Identifiers: LCCN: 2020912630 | ISBN 9780998032139 (pbk.) | 9780998032146 (e-book)

Subjects: LCSH Healing — Meditations. | Christian life. | Devotional literature. | Grief — Religious aspects — Christianity. | Bereavement — Religious aspects — Christianity. | Loss (Psychology) — Religious aspects — Christianity. | Suffering — Religious aspects — Christianity. | Prayers and devotions. | BISAC RELIGION / Christian Living / Devotional | RELIGION / Christian Ministry / Counseling & Recovery | SELF-HELP / Post-Traumatic Stress Disorder (PTSD)

Classification: LCC BV4905.3 .T87 2020 | DDC 242/.4 — dc23

Table of Contents

Foreword

I LOVE WORDS, and I love well written devotional literature. Both represent my calling and livelihood. But what I love the most is a well-lived life—forged in the furnace of disruption, honest struggle, and a thirst for more of God's grace. That's why Elizabeth's words carry weight, and why these meditations are much more than nice devotional thoughts with which to begin, or end, a busy day.

We have walked with Elizabeth and Kip Turnage, as couples and friends, for many years. Years marked by fun and laughter, for sure, and no small amount of fine food. But more importantly, years in which providence has sometimes proven difficult, circumstances less than polite, and our shared need for more of the Gospel an uncontested reality. What more could we want in friendship?

So as I read though these sixty meditations, I remember specific stories, and unrushed conversations; burden bearing care, and mutual encouragement. Indeed, these meditations were written with the ink of sharing life, before the tapping of computer keys.

By the cover and title, Elizabeth makes it clear, she has written meditations for those in an ongoing journey; not formulas for those looking for a magic pill, easy answers, or functional spin. Restoration continues; resolution awaits us. Life between the resurrection and return of Jesus inevitably involves traveling through many crises and crucibles. Peace and hope are very possible, but they are not inevitable.

What we do with our pain? Where do we go for peace? To whom or what do we look for hope? Whom do we allow to narrate our stories? These are the questions Elizabeth invites us to ponder in these sixty meditations. Jesus never promised us a storm-free life. But he *has* promised us we'll never experience a Christ-absent day. Elizabeth has found Jesus in the storms of life. She invites us to know his pursuit and presence.

Meditation is much different than reading. Meditation engages head and heart. If you are in a hurry, you can blow through this book in one sitting. Don't make getting through this book a project. Receive it as an invitation. Go through it at the pace of grace. Time alone heals nothing. We just grow more calluses. Time plus grace is the heartbeat of the Gospel. Make the time, and God will supply the grace.

SCOTTY SMITH
PASTOR EMERITUS, CHRIST COMMUNITY CHURCH, FRANKLIN, TN
TEACHER IN RESIDENCE, WEST END COMMUNITY CHURCH, NASHVILLE, TN

Preface

IF YOU'RE READING THIS, you've likely known the crushing of a crisis, the shattering of a devastated dream, the fragmenting that comes from a broken relationship, or the abrupt end to something—or someone—precious.

I too have experienced the radical altering of my story through crisis. When I began to write this devotional, the global pandemic of the coronavirus had not yet begun—but even before the coronavirus turned our world upside-down, I had limped through the journey of crisis and recovery multiple times.

My parents divorced when I was only seven years old; healing is ongoing. When I was twelve, a bicycle crash shattered my elbow in twenty-five places, landing me in the hospital for three weeks; my left arm still throbs with the lasting impact. As a teenager, I experienced sexual abuse by men in authority over me; their improper advances carved scars that remain today.

As an adult, I've lived through disaster recovery after our city was gutted by a category four hurricane. I've undergone ten major orthopedic surgeries in the past fifteen years. I've cared for my husband when he was hospitalized for ten days with a life-threatening condition, and for our younger son when he was diagnosed with a brain tumor at twenty-two and endured four brain surgeries in a nine-month window.

I know what it feels like to have your story shorn by one phone call, one accident, one natural disaster. I know what it feels like to grieve the losses that come through the shearing. And I know what it feels like to wait, seemingly forever, to return to a new normal.

But I also know this. Because Jesus endured the crisis of the cross for us, and because he was raised from the dead, we have certain hope of full restoration. If your story has been shattered by crisis, please read on.

Introduction

IF YOU'VE EVER BEEN in a recovery room, especially if you've been there more than once, you know that the return passage from anesthesia is not always a gentle stroll down a garden path. You also know that the hours passed in the recovery room, where kind and skilled medical personnel tend to your every need, can be a walk in the park compared to the wilderness journey of recovery that stretches ahead.

CRISIS

When you find yourself lying in a recovery room, it's because your body has undergone a crisis of sorts, "a radical change of status."[1] Chemically induced to numbness and sleep, it has undergone the intrusion of a surgeon's scalpel. Now it must recover in order to return to a normal state of breathing and consciousness and activity. In the same way, recovery in our lives follows some kind of crisis, some kind of radical altering of the state of things, often a "difficult or dangerous state that needs serious attention."[2]

A house flooded, cancer diagnosed, a baby miscarried, justice miscarried. Abandoned by a husband, betrayed by a business partner, abused by a volleyball coach. Faith forsaken by a daughter, hope crushed by addiction, love stolen by death. Such crises can plunge us into a state of chaos and confusion, disorder and depression. Shalom has been shattered, equilibrium lost. Despair threatens hope. Strife assaults peace. What we yearn for is a return to normal, a way to regain what was lost in the crisis. A recovery.

FROM RECOVERY TO RESTORATION

Although we may find our way to a new normal after a crisis, we may never fully regain what we lost in the shattering. My shoulders will always ache despite two surgeries on one and three on the other. Your husband may marry the woman he had an affair with. Your child was not raised from the dead like the widow's son. And yet, there may be hope.

In literature, crisis refers to a turning point in the story. What if our crisis presents a turning point in our story? What if our season in recovery leads us to unearth treasure even richer than what we lost? Scripture suggests that God has something more for us in crisis and recovery. What if we discovered the genuine hope of final restoration in our recovery? What if we could discover…

- Restored trust in the God who allowed this suffering?

- Recognition of our profound need for a Savior who has rescued us from sin?

- Renewal of our hearts, souls, bodies, and minds, so that we may live and love like Jesus?

- Our richest restoration hope: the promise that one day Jesus will return and restore all broken things.

The good news of the gospel is that God is writing just such stories of redemption and restoration as we walk through crisis and recovery. God is taking us beyond recovery to restoration.

BEYOND RECOVERY: THE RESTORATION STORY OF SCRIPTURE

In the restoration story of Scripture, we discover the basis for our peace and hope.

Creation: In the beginning, God created the cosmos to flourish. He created man and woman in his image, to bring him glory by exercising dominion over the good world he had created. Humans were designed to be fruitful and multiply, to enjoy God, to enjoy one another, and to enjoy God's good creation. Joy and glory were intertwined in all of life in a state of harmony and flourishing called "shalom" (Genesis 1-2).

Fall: The serpent, Satan embodied, slinked into the garden, seducing Eve and Adam, drawing them into his untrue tale of God's dubious goodness. It was the first crisis, the first turning point, in the Bible. Adam and Eve, presented with an opportunity to trust God and do as he had commanded them, made a disastrous choice.

They ate of the only tree in the garden forbidden them by their extravagant Creator. When they did, all the d's of disaster entered the world: death, division, despoiling, demeaning, disease, and so on. This crisis thrust Adam and Eve, and all of their future heirs, into recovery. A cut was made, sin and shame were exposed, and death descended. Shalom was shattered. Now all humans would require revival and recovery (Genesis 3).

Redemption: Thanks be to God, the story did not end in this crisis. Even before the beginning of time as we know it, God had planned to move into the disaster caused by Adam and Eve's sin (Ephesians 1:4). He invited them to come to him, to confess their sin to him. He pursued them in their shame (Genesis 3:9). He pronounced the curses and consequences that would follow their disobedience (Genesis 3:9-19).

At the same time, he gave them temporary relief, exchanging their flimsy fig-leaf covers for the skins of animals sacrificed for them. He announced that he would one day send a Savior, who in the worst crisis of world history, would die on a cross, cursed for sins he didn't commit (Genesis 3:16). And then, he exiled them from the garden, protecting them from eternal existence in the sinful state they had chosen (Genesis 3:20-24).

In the paradox of paradoxes, God allowed the death of his Son to revive our sinners' hearts. Through Christ's death and resurrection, God's people are redeemed, the blood of his body covering our sins, his death paying its brutal price. Through his death, Christ reconciled us to God, clothed us in his righteousness, and made us new creation (2 Corinthians 5:17-21). He began the restoration of the shalom the prophets foresaw as being completed one day.

Restoration: One day we will know the full restoration of shalom the prophets dreamed of. Cornelius Plantinga describes this fully restored shalom:

> They dreamed of a time when the deserts would flower, the mountains would run with wine, weeping would cease, and people could go to sleep without weapons on their laps.
>
> People would work in peace and work to fruitful effect. Lambs could lie down with lions. All nature would be fruitful, benign, and filled with wonder upon wonder.
>
> All humans would be knit together in brotherhood and sisterhood; and all nature and all humans would

look to God, walk with God, lean toward God, and delight in God.

Shouts of joy and recognition would well up from valleys and seas, from women in streets and from men on ships. The webbing together of God, humans, and all creation in justice, fulfillment, and delight is what the Hebrew prophets call shalom.[3]

According to Revelation, the prophets' predictions will materialize. One day, "soon," Jesus will return and restore all things broken in the crisis of the fall (Revelation 22:7). We will cheer and we will hug as we are reunited with our heavenly bridegroom, as we recover loved ones lost too early to death. We will rejoice over our new home in the heavenly city, the new Jerusalem established right here on earth. The image of God will finally be fully restored in us, and we will shine with his glory. We will eagerly serve Christ as he rules over the cosmos, and we will give unceasing praise to our Creator and Redeemer for his restoration work. In that day, we will be beyond the need for recovery; we will be fully restored (Revelation 21-22).

Dear friends, because of the good news of the gospel, we do have every reason to hope. Join me in the journey beyond recovery, to discover the riches of his restoration.

How This Book Is Designed

MEDITATIONS FOR PEACE AND HOPE

ALTHOUGH MEDITATION HAS gained popularity in the twenty-first century as a means of achieving calm, God encouraged it first long ago. The Bible uses the word *meditate* to refer to the practice of going over the works of God and the Word of God in your mind. The Hebrew word literally means to "chew on," as a cow chews its cud, or as a dog gnaws on a bone. We are to let God's Word marinate in our hearts, captivate our thoughts, and integrate our lives. As we meditate on God's Word, our hearts ease, we fix our hopes on the certain future to come, and we know the peace that surpasses all understanding. The meditations in these pages are arranged according to some of the varied topics, experiences, and emotions you might encounter during a season of recovery from crisis.

SCRIPTURE

Each meditation begins with a Bible verse. Read it over several times—aloud if you dare. If you have time, read the verses suggested at the end of each meditation under "Further Encouragement."

PRAYER

When we are in crisis, we may struggle to find the words or the concentration to pray. Use the short prayer at the end of each meditation to get started. Consider also writing prayers out in a prayer journal. No matter what approach you take, remember that the Lord loves to hear your prayers and to answer them with his Word of hope.

FURTHER ENCOURAGEMENT

Each meditation includes suggestions for further reading, listening, or action: Bible reading, prayers, music. Playlists for the songs may be found at www.elizabethturnage.com/From RecoverytoRestoration.

FOR REFLECTION

At the end of each meditation, you will find a question for reflection and journaling.

APPENDIX

Here you will find additional suggestions for finding peace and hope as you wait: further reading, exercises, and playlists.

1

Be of Good Cheer

*These things I have spoken to you, that
in Me you may have peace. In the world
you will have tribulation; but be of good
cheer, I have overcome the world.*
JOHN 16:33, NKJV

HERE ON THE Gulf Coast of Florida, hurricane season threatens every year, tossing its mighty winds and roaring waters through our mind's eye, arousing fears of future devastation and memories of past disaster. It's been about fifteen years since Hurricane Ivan wreaked its havoc on our hometown, Pensacola, Florida, leaving a swath of blue roofs in its wake.

We've recovered. But some never did. Some lost homes, businesses, even marriages to the disaster. They may have found a new home or started a new business, but the heartache of the catastrophe lingers. Maybe you haven't been hit by a hurricane; maybe it was a divorce, a sudden revelation of a spouse's affair. Maybe you were slapped with a cancer diagnosis. Or maybe your twenty-three-year-old has just renounced her faith.

The hard reality is that in this life we may never fully recover from some disasters we endure. How can we live with hope in a world in which some losses will never be recouped? Jesus, in his final words to his disciples, anticipated this question. Shortly before his brutal crucifixion for a trumped-up crime, he prepared his followers for the disasters that mark life in a fallen world:

"In the world you will have tribulation; but be of good cheer, for I have overcome the world" (John 16:33 NKJV).

Jesus' words confound many of us, because western culture has fed us a lie: "This world is all there is," it tells us, "and the things in it are here to make us happy." Jesus contradicted this lie, telling his disciples something like this, "Yes, in this world, you will suffer. I'm teaching you how to live in *my* world, *my* kingdom. Not only that, when I die and am raised again, you will have the resurrection power to live a different life, a new life, to begin to recover what was lost in the fall. When you suffer, remember these things I have told you, and you will have peace. Not only that, you can be 'of good cheer,' 'take courage,' 'not be afraid,' 'take heart'—because 'I have overcome the world.'"

One day, not yet, but "soon," Jesus said, "I will return" (Revelation 22:7). In that day, we will live with him in a new world, the world we were really made for. In that day, all of the pain and sorrow of the disasters we have faced will be washed away. All the sin—the clawing to get our own way, the clashing against loved ones over minor differences, the clinging to things we think will satisfy—it will be over. Overcome. Defeated. By him—our King.

Dear friends, let's take heart. There is something better that awaits. It is beyond recovery. It is restoration. It is renewal. It is reunion. Cheer loudly and long. Jesus has overcome the world.

Lord Jesus,

Thank you for setting us straight. We are far too focused on finding joy in the things of this world. Help us to trust you when we suffer, to know that in you alone we will find peace and hope. In your cheering name we pray. AMEN.

FURTHER ENCOURAGEMENT

- Read John 16.

- Listen to "What a Friend" by Sara Groves.

FOR REFLECTION

What hope do you find in Jesus' words to his disciples?

NOTES

2

Landscape of Loss

For we know that all creation has been
groaning as in the pains of childbirth
right up to the present time.
ROMANS 8:22, NLT

AFTER HURRICANE IVAN wreaked its havoc on our hometown, Pensacola, Florida, I described our world as a "landscape of loss." Perhaps that three-word phrase seems to describe the current state of your marriage, your family, your work, your relationships, or your health. You are not alone. Ever since the fall, the entire creation has become a landscape of loss, groaning to be restored.

When God created the cosmos, he declared it *good*. When he created Adam and Eve, he declared them *very good*. While God richly and abundantly provided for Adam and Eve and all of creation, he placed one limitation on their freedom. He instructed them not to eat of the tree of the knowledge of good and evil. He didn't give them a reason. He didn't have to, because he was their Creator and Sustainer. They had no reason to doubt his loving provision.

But then Satan, embodying the serpent, entered the scene, planting seeds of doubt. Satan implied that God was holding out on them. Adam, standing right there next to Eve, remained silent. Eve looked at the tree and saw that it was pleasing to the eye and desirable to make her wise. She ate and "gave some to her husband, who was with her" (Genesis 3:1–6).

In that moment, creation began its groaning, and its groaning continues today. It echoes through our anguished cries:

- Why did your husband become entangled with another woman? Because, on that long-ago day, marriage, which God had designed to last forever, was split by a divide that would reach, through sin's tentacles, into today (Genesis 3:7).

- Why does your teen-aged daughter stare murderously at her peas when you try to engage her in dinner table conversation? Because on that long-ago day, the joy of bearing and raising children would bring with it a curse of relational pain that we still feel today (Genesis 3:16).

- Why did you get laid off after faithfully working sixty hours a week for the last thirty years? Because on that long-ago day, the ground that Adam worked became cursed, and all work became fraught with frustration (Genesis 3:17).

And on and on we could go, because in the fall, man's sin had catastrophic effects on all of creation. If you are living in a landscape of loss, there is a reason.

And yet, there is hope. Because even as everything came crashing down, God moved toward his sinful yet beloved creation. He pronounced the curses and consequences of their sin, yes, but he also announced the gospel for the first time. He warned Satan that one day, Christ would come to crush all evil and sin (Genesis 3:15). Yes, there is hope. One day, creation's agonized cries will be transformed into agonies of delight.

PRAYER

Creator God,

We cry with all of creation, longing for the day when our sin will cease, longing for the day when Christ will return and restore all things. In Christ's redeeming name. AMEN.

FURTHER ENCOURAGEMENT

- Read Genesis 3:1–24.

- Listen to "Mercy Leads" by Sisters.

FOR REFLECTION

In what way does the world around you resemble a "landscape of loss"? What would restoration look like?

NOTES

3

Telling It Like It Is: Lament

*Cry aloud before the Lord, O walls of beautiful
Jerusalem! Let your tears flow day and night.
Give yourselves no rest; Give your eyes no relief.*
LAMENTATIONS 2:19, ESV

GRIEF EXPERTS ENCOURAGE victims to name their losses, because doing so facilitates recovery. Scripture seems to agree, for it abounds with lament, vivid expressions of grief and complaint to the Lord about a shattered world. Lamentations, Job, and over thirty percent of the Psalms are characterized by biblical lament.

Biblical lament usually follows a pattern of turning to God, naming the grief, asking for help, and renewing confidence in God. As Joni Eareckson Tada, a quadriplegic who has been confined to a wheelchair for over fifty years, explains, the pro-cess of lament transforms our hearts: "Sorrow and sin must always be faced head on. It is this no-nonsense, raw approach that allows hope to grow in the fertile ground left from the ashes of suffering."[4]

Lamentations, an entire book devoted to Jeremiah's lament over the devastating fall of Jerusalem, helps us to develop a language of lament. Let's consider the four aspects of lament demonstrated by Jeremiah, the probable author of Lamentations.

1. *Turning to God:* Sometimes we turn away from God in disaster. We simply don't know what to say to him, so we say nothing. We avoid him, avoiding Scripture, avoiding church, avoiding Christians. In Lamentations, Jeremiah turns toward God, addressing him directly.

2. *Naming the grief to God:* Jeremiah refuses to minimize the suffering of Jerusalem: "I am the one who has seen the afflictions that come from the rod of the Lord's anger. He has led me into darkness, shutting out all light" (Lamentations 3:1 NLT). Jeremiah and other biblical lamenters articulate their grief to God, noting how their current experience doesn't seem to match their understanding of God's goodness and mercy.

3. *Asking persistently and boldly for help:* Jeremiah cries out, "Let them lie face down in the dust for there may be hope at last" (Lamentations 3:29 NLT). In other words, keep mourning until an answer comes. His boldness comes from his confidence that "no one is abandoned by the Lord forever" (Lamentations 3:31 NLT).

4. *Expressing restored confidence:* Not always (see Psalm 88), but often, there is a turn in lament, in which the lamenter remembers God's goodness and expresses his confidence that the Lord will redeem and restore again. It is this renewed hope that gives birth to the oft-quoted lines from the book of Lamentations:

"But this I call to mind, and therefore I have hope:

The steadfast love of the Lord never ceases; his mercies never come to an end. They are new every morning; great is your faithfulness" (Lamentations 3:21–23).

Dear friends, do not be shy about naming your losses. Direct them toward God, who invites you to grieve with him. As you engage in lament, you will discover anew the God whose faithfulness is great, whose steadfast love never ceases.

PRAYER

Father,

Forgive us for turning away from you in our grief, for pretending that we don't hurt. Thank you for inviting us to lament. Restore our hearts even as we cry out to you. In Jesus' weeping name, we pray. AMEN.

FURTHER ENCOURAGEMENT

- Read Lamentations 1–5.

- Listen to "Come Lift Up Your Sorrows" by Michael Card.

FOR REFLECTION

Try writing out a biblical lament. Include all four aspects: turning to God, naming your grief to God, asking God for help, and expressing restored confidence in him. After doing this, journal about what this process was like for you.

NOTES

4

His Mercies Are New

The steadfast love of the Lord never ceases; His
mercies never come to an end; They are new
every morning; Great is your faithfulness.
LAMENTATIONS 3:22–23, ESV

"WHERE WILL I LIVE? How will I get a job? How will I stay sober?" These are just a few of the questions posed by women in our jail Bible study when they face the "hopeful" prospect of being released. The obstacles they face in recovery are many, seemingly impossible to overcome. They are not alone. In a season of recovery, we all need to call to mind God's steadfast love and new morning mercies. As we do, we will discover the hope that anchors us for today and encourages us for tomorrow.

Jeremiah puts words to God's new morning mercies in the aftermath of Babylon's destruction of Jerusalem. Surrounded by the shattered remnants of the once beautiful "city of peace," Jeremiah points to God as the party responsible for driving him into darkness (Lamentations 3:2), making his "flesh and skin waste away," and enveloping him with "bitterness and tribulation" (Lamentations 3:4–5). And yet, even in this state of intense agony, Jeremiah remembers the steadfast and unceasing love of the Lord, the mercies that are new every morning, and he has hope.

We, like Jeremiah, need to recall that God's mercy is new and fitting every day. Each day, whatever trouble we face, we know that God's new mercy will reliably show itself, providing what we need.

- When we don't know how we will get through physical therapy today because we're so worn out from a pain-plagued night:
  His mercies are new, energizing us with the strength to do our exercises.

- When we don't know how we will make it through the court proceedings for our daughter's arrest:
  His mercies are new, holding us up when we feel like falling down.

- When we don't know what we will do about all the bills we can't pay at the end of the month:
  His mercies are new, giving us the wisdom we need and showing us where to turn for help.

- When we don't know how we will endure one more day of being left by the one we loved:
  His mercies are new, surrounding us with the comfort of his Holy Spirit, speaking tenderly to us through his Word.

- When we have relapsed, fallen back into the sinful pit that has already brought disaster:
  His mercies are new, reminding us of his forgiveness in

Jesus Christ, giving us the peace that accompanies that forgiveness.

Whatever trouble you face today, turn to your faithful Father, whose mercy is great. Look to him who has already provided "pardon for sin and a peace that endureth" to see how he will give you "strength for today and bright hope for tomorrow."[5]

PRAYER

Father God,

Great indeed is your faithfulness. Help us to take each day as it comes, knowing that your new morning mercies will be sufficient for every specific need. By your mercy in your Son, we pray. AMEN.

FURTHER ENCOURAGEMENT

- Read Lamentations 3:1–27.

- Listen to "Great Is Thy Faithfulness" by Austin Stone Worship.

FOR REFLECTION

Make a list of the troubles you face today or in the days to come. Consider how God might meet you in those troubles with his new morning mercies.

5

Do Not Fear

Fear not, for I have redeemed you; I have
called you by name, you are mine.
ISAIAH 43:1, ESV

WHETHER THE CRISIS comes in the form of a wildfire roaring down the mountain or a river rising near your home, whether the crisis comes in the form of divorce papers arriving at your door or addiction landing you in a wreck, one of your earliest responses may be shock and fear. Into your frenzy, the Lord offers reason for calm.

Isaiah speaks the hopeful words, "Fear not," even as he foretells the crisis God's people, the Israelites, will face. Despite God's warnings through his prophets, Israel has persistently rebelled against God. Their sins are about to bring disaster: Babylon will destroy their sacred home, and they will be exiled to a pagan nation. In the face of the coming terror, the Lord reassures them: "Fear not, for I have redeemed you; I have called you by name, you are mine" (Isaiah 43:1b).

Although the crises we face may differ from the Israelites', the reasons for peace and hope in the midst still apply. Why should we "fear not"? Listen, as God speaks over his people, over you, these hopeful words:

- "I will be with you" (Isaiah 43:2). When you feel you will drown in grief, be consumed by the loss, remember your reason to hope—Christ is in you by his Spirit.

- "You are precious in my eyes, and honored, and I love you" (Isaiah 43:4). When you doubt his love because of the troubles mounting on every side, remember that God sent his Son to die for you, because you are precious to him.

- "[I will] bring my sons from afar, and my daughters from the end of the earth" (Isaiah 43:6). When you feel that the exile and isolation of this season will never end, remember that Christ was separated from God so you might be reunited to him.

- "I have called you by name, you are mine" (Isaiah 43:1). When you feel despised, abandoned, or orphaned by your losses, remember that Jesus was despised, abandoned, and orphaned so you might be called by God's name.

Even as you shudder with the shock of your situation, let the Lord's words wash over you. He created you, forming you even in the womb, for his glory, and he is redeeming you, bringing you back to him, through this severe mercy.

PRAYER

Lord God,

We confess our fears, doubts, and struggles to you. Thank you for bringing certainty amid our confusion. Help us remember that we belong to you, that we are not orphans, that you will never leave us. Help us to rest in the tender hope that we are precious to you. In Jesus' redeeming name. AMEN.

FURTHER ENCOURAGEMENT

- Read Isaiah 43:1–7.

- Listen to "Abide with Me" by Audrey Assad.

FOR REFLECTION

How have you felt shock or confusion in this crisis? Read the words of Isaiah 43:1–7 aloud and rest in the peace offered.

NOTES

6

Revive My Soul

My soul clings to the dust; give me
life according to your word!
PSALM 119:25, ESV

IN ONE MOMENT, one hour, one day, perhaps, your life has
been radically altered. So altered that you're not sure you'll
survive. When your world has been tossed like a rag doll in a
tornado, where do you turn?

The writer of Psalm 119 tells us: we must turn to the Word,
which revives and restores our souls. In this vast 176-verse ode
to the Word, the psalmist catalogues the circumstances of life
which sent him there and proclaims the abounding blessings
he discovered there. From him, we can learn how the Word
rights us when our world is not right.

Even as the psalmist declares his love for Scripture, he also
names the desperate need which drove him there. Maybe you
can relate. Among the trials he mentions in Psalm 119, he has
experienced exile on earth, "scorn and contempt", soul-melt-
ing sorrow, and the dread of reproach (Psalm 119:19, 22, 28,
39). His soul "clings to the dust," perhaps because of the "evil-
minded people" who have lied about him (Psalm 119:25, 115,

78 NLT). He has been ensnared by the wicked and known the faithful affliction of the Lord (Psalm 119:110, 75). He has been oppressed, persecuted, and despised (Psalm 119:121, 161, 141). And he has gone astray like a lost sheep (Psalm 119:176).

The Lord responds to his desperate need, and the psalmist declares his fervent devotion to the Word. As he details the ways the Word has restored and revived him, we see how it will restore and revive us in seasons of recovery:

- The Word counsels and clarifies, lighting our way when we walk in darkness (Psalm 119:105). It exposes "false ways of life" and leads us away from them (Psalm 119:104 NLT).

- The Word stabilizes and secures, revealing God's steadfast love and faithfulness in our trouble (Psalm 119:75–77). "Firmly fixed in the heavens," the Word reminds us of the unchangeable nature of God in the midst of a changing world (Psalm 119:89).

- The Word saves and delivers, acting as our "refuge and shield" against "evil-minded people" (Psalm 119:114–115 NLT). The Word's rules give life even as its commands bring freedom (Psalm 119:93, 45).

- Finally, and most importantly, the Word restores and revives us. It fills us with hope when we are afflicted; it raises us to new life when we are groveling in the dust (Psalm 119:49, 25). The Word gives us life by turning our eyes away from "worthless things"; the Word gives us life by reminding us of God's promises (Psalm 119:37, 50).

Dear friends, if your world has been turned upside down or split wide open, keep reaching for the Word. There you will find the peace and hope you need.

PRAYER

Lord,

We confess — sometimes the last thing we reach for in crisis is your Word. Help us to read first and react later. Grow in us a love and longing for the Word that gives us the life we crave. In the name of Jesus, the Word-made-flesh, we ask. AMEN.

FURTHER ENCOURAGEMENT

- Read Psalm 119 over a period of several days.

- Listen to "Speak, O Lord" by Keith and Kristyn Getty.

FOR REFLECTION

As you read Psalm 119, underline or write down words that particularly resonate with you—for example, *perish*, *revive*, *contempt*, or *delight*. Then write a letter to God using some of those words to tell him how you are feeling and ask him to meet you in his Word.

NOTES

7

Waiting or Whining?

I wait for the Lord, my soul waits,
And in his word I hope....
PSALM 130:5, ESV

"WHY DOES SHE get to graduate from PT when she's only been here for two months, and I've been here for six?" My physical therapist responded kindly but firmly, "Not every shoulder surgery is the same. Some people have easier recoveries." I turned my back on him and stuck out my tongue. Real mature. I was, without a doubt, becoming whiny in my wait to recover.

When we've been the victim of a crisis, we can easily turn to victimization as a way of life. Self-help and self-pity may look like the way out of our distress, but they often lead to more whining and less waiting on the Lord. In Psalm 130, David shows us the way out of the whine.

He cries out to the Lord from the depths of despair. Although not all suffering is a consequence of our own sin — David has suffered from the brutal betrayal of King Saul as well as his enemies' attacks — in Psalm 130, David is crying out for forgiveness. David recognizes the drop-down knockout power of his own sin, "If you, O Lord, should mark iniquities, who could stand?" (Psalm 130:3). He knows the Lord's forgiveness for his sin is a sure cure for his worst injury.

As we wait for healing from a harmful loss or a painful injury, as we wait for homes to be rebuilt or hearts to be renewed, David teaches us how to wait well:

> I wait for the Lord, my soul waits,
> And in his word I hope;
> My soul waits for the Lord,
> More than watchmen wait for the morning,
> More than watchmen wait for the morning
> (Psalm 130:6).

To wait well, we must learn to turn our eyes away from ourselves and toward the Lord. We must become good watchmen for the Lord, seeking him in the darkness, certain that he will come soon, sure that his arrival will bring relief. As Jill Carrattini writes, we have every reason to hope as we wait, for "Christ himself can transform our watching and our waiting, our lives and our deaths, bringing light where death stings, tears discourage, and darkness haunts: the Light has already come!"[6]

When our focus in waiting shifts from recouping losses to recognizing redemption, we see even more reason to hope, "For with the Lord there is steadfast love, and with him is plentiful redemption" (Psalm 130:7). As you endure this hard wait, keep watching for the Lord. In him, you will find the help you need for all of your distress.

Lord,

We confess, we often become whiny as we wait for recovery. Help us, we pray, to see your plentiful redemption, to seek your forgiveness for our sins. Turn our faces toward you and help us see the dawn which has already arrived in our Savior Jesus Christ. In his very near name, we ask. AMEN.

FURTHER ENCOURAGEMENT

- Read Psalm 130.
- Listen to "I Will Wait for You" by Shane and Shane.

FOR REFLECTION

Have you found yourself moving toward self-pity, or have you noticed yourself whining in your wait for recovery? What has that looked like? Write or say a prayer of confession and thank God for his mercy.

NOTES

8

Darkness Overcome

The people who walked in darkness
have seen a great light.
ISAIAH 9:2, ESV

FAMILIES AND FRIENDS were divided. The land had been ravaged. The economy was in turmoil, and the political system was corrupt. Such was the disastrous condition of God's chosen nation, Israel, in 725 B.C., when Isaiah wrote. The people walked in "distress and darkness," in the "gloom of anguish" (Isaiah 8:22). Isaiah brought good news for the people of Israel and for us today as we walk in the dark shadows of crisis: a brilliant light has shone into this thick darkness, dispelling the gloom.

What is this great light? We know now what Isaiah could only see from a distance. This light is the light of a newborn babe, the "life that was the light of men" (John 1:4). When the babe, God-with-us (Immanuel), was born, the people who had walked in the darkness of God's silence for four hundred years saw a star shining in the east. This bright star pointed to a brighter glory, the glorious light of God-made-flesh that "shines in the darkness," the light that the darkness cannot overcome (John 1:5).

This babe, the child of God, would be called "Wonderful Counselor, Mighty God, Everlasting Father, Prince of Peace" (Isaiah 9:6). He would overcome the darkness with his powerful and purifying light:

Making our burdens light by shouldering our sin and throwing off our oppressors (Isaiah 9:4).

Increasing peace in our hearts, in our lives, and in his cosmos by burning weapons of war and restoring order to chaos and confusion (Isaiah 9:5).

Shining glory from a crown that rules over all nations and draws multitudes to bow before him (Isaiah 9:3, 7).

Governing with the light of justice and righteousness established "from this time forth and forevermore" (Isaiah 9:7).

Isaiah understood that those who walked in darkness could never see this great light on their own. The black hole of their rebellion had so blinded them that it would take the mighty work of a majestic God to open their eyes. Into this dark reality came more good news: "The zeal of the Lord of hosts will do this" (Isaiah 9:7). Our God's zealous love, his passionate intensity and his jealous desire for his people, compelled him to send his saving Light into the world. He is the "God-of-Angel-Armies," (Isaiah 9:7 MSG), and he has commanded all of his heavenly and earthly battalions to open our eyes to the light of life that overcomes our darkness.

Dear friends, what cause for rejoicing we have when we feel enveloped by thick darkness. His light has shone into this darkness, and "the darkness has not overcome it" (John 1:5). Let's keep looking to the horizon of hope, where his new mercies dawn every day. Let's keep looking to the horizon of hope, to see the Son of righteousness who will one day rise with forever healing in his wings (Malachi 4:2).

PRAYER

Glorious God,

Some days the "gloom of anguish" threatens to overwhelm us. Thank you for sending the Light of life into this world and for opening our eyes to see your Son, our Savior, who has overcome the darkness. In Jesus' brilliant name. AMEN.

FURTHER ENCOURAGEMENT

- Read Isaiah 9:1–7; John 1:1–18.
- Listen to "To the Dawn" by Sara Groves.

FOR REFLECTION

Have you had the sense of being enveloped by darkness in this crisis? How have you seen Jesus' light shine hope into dark places?

NOTES

9

Scan-xiety, Triggers, and Aftershocks

He heals the brokenhearted and
binds up their wounds.
PSALM 147:3, ESV

DESPITE BEING FIVE years cancer-free, my friend always breaks out into hives before her yearly PET-scan. Twenty-five years after a tornado wrecked our neighborhood, my adult daughters still experience anxiety about tornado warnings. After five shoulder surgeries in a two-year period, my body trembled uncontrollably at every physical therapy appointment.

You may have nightmares, panic attacks, or other seemingly inexplicable physical responses in unexpected moments. You are experiencing a normal response to a radically life-altering event. God has wired our brains and bodies exquisitely; traumatic events can cause psychological dysfunction that needs to be healed just as a broken bone needs to be set. Thankfully, our loving God has created multiple resources for healing the brokenhearted and binding up our psychological and emotional wounds. Consider these resources that many have found helpful:

- *Memorizing and meditating on Scripture (Psalm 48:9):* A friend with breast cancer takes a set of Scripture cards with her to every oncologist appointment. Focusing on the words of hope helps to still and calm her mind.

- *Prayer (1 Thessalonians 5:17):* A recently divorced mother of three struggles with worry spinning out of control at night. When the spinning begins, she turns on the bedside lamp and writes a prayer, telling God everything she is worried about and asking him to ease her mind.

- *Fixing our eyes on Jesus and on true and lovely things (Hebrews 12:1; Philippians 4:8):* As my physical therapist performs the painful procedure of scraping away at scar tissue, I combat the pain by picturing Jesus gathering the little children to him. Setting our minds on things above can distract us from pain (Colossians 3:2).

- *Remembering God's rescue in the past and envisioning our future hope (Psalm 35:10; Isaiah 43:1):* Two years after the 500-year-flood in Pensacola left six feet of water in her home, a friend began to have nightmares about her house being flooded again. She began writing down the many ways God had helped her family during the actual flood and pictured the day when Jesus would come back to heal all of broken creation. This exercise helped her return to sleep.

- *Seeking good counsel (Proverbs 15:22):* In addition to seeking the counsel of Scripture, we can seek the counsel of skilled counselors who know how to help us deal with post-traumatic stress. A friend who suffered panic attacks years after being sexually abused obtained the help of a professional counselor. This wise and well-trained counselor knew the science of how God had wired her brain and body and knew how to help her heal.

Dear friends, if you are suffering the symptoms of post-traumatic stress, be as patient with yourself as your loving Physician is. The one who formed you in the womb understands your every response, and he stands ready to send resources to bind up your wounds and heal your broken heart.

PRAYER

Lord,

Sometimes we feel crazy for the way we are reacting. Give us patience with ourselves and direct us to the help we need in this season of stress. In Jesus' calming name. AMEN.

FURTHER ENCOURAGEMENT

- Read Psalm 48:9; 1 Thessalonians 5:17; Hebrews 12:1; Philippians 4:8; Psalm 35:10; Isaiah 43:1; Proverbs 15:22.

- Listen to "Be Still My Soul" by Kari Jobe.

FOR REFLECTION

List any symptoms of post-traumatic stress you have experienced. What places, objects, people, words, etc. do you recognize as triggering that stress? What has helped you in dealing with these symptoms? What further help might you seek?

NOTES

10

Throwing Off Anxiety

Cast all your anxiety on him
because he cares for you.
1 PETER 5:7, NIV

WHEN OUR SON was diagnosed with a brain tumor, there were times that anxiety clutched at my chest and clawed at my stomach, even when my mind and heart felt at peace with God. In crisis and even long after a crisis has passed, it's not unusual for our bodies to experience such symptoms of anxiety.[7] But when it creeps in, we can learn to cast our anxiety onto the Lord, who is so full of care for us.

As we combat anxiety, we must realize that it won't always slip easily off our shoulders; we must actively "cast" it. We need to take that weighty sack of worries and heave it on the Lord, who beckons us to come to him with our heavy burdens (Matthew 11:28). How do we go about throwing off our heavy burden of anxiety? As we pray and study Scripture, we can also keep in mind four things Peter mentions.

First, we can recognize that Satan prowls around our distress (1 Peter 5:8), seeking to stir up anxiety. He enjoys tempting us, especially to doubt God's goodness. He enjoys accusing us of failing miserably. As we become "sober-minded; watchful" (1 Peter 5:8) and "resist him, standing firm in the faith" (1 Peter 5:9), he will flee from us (James 4:7). As Satan flees, so will much of our anxiety.

Second, we can remember that we are not alone in suffering (1 Peter 5:9). Anxiety often stems from and feeds into a sense of isolation. We begin to believe that no one could possibly understand what it's like to—lose a baby, go through such a miserable breakup, or be laid off at age fifty-five. Or, we buy into the lie that no one can help us out of this disaster. As we recall that suffering is normal for Christians and as we allow others to bear our burdens (Galatians 6:2), we cast our anxiety on the Lord.

Third, we can stand firm in the faith (1 Peter 5:9). Our faith in God in the present is strengthened by our memory of his "mighty acts" and "awesome deeds" in the past (Psalm 145:4, 6). He parted the Red Sea to rescue the Israelites from the Egyptians; will he not also rescue and sustain us in the midst of disaster? Long ago, because he loved us, he sent his Son, Jesus, to the cross to redeem us; will he not continue his redemptive work today? As we remember God's might and mercy, our minds calm; our anxiety eases.

Finally, we can look to God's promises for the future. Today's suffering *will* end; in fact, over the long haul, it will only seem to have lasted for a "little while" (2 Peter 5:10). Not only will it end, it will end in "eternal glory in Christ," when the "God of all grace… will himself restore, confirm, strengthen, and establish you" (2 Peter 5:10). Now that's a heavy promise for heaving off anxiety!

PRAYER

Father,

As anxiety rises, help us to keep tossing it off,
remembering your redemption, looking forward
to the future day when all of your promises will be
fulfilled. AMEN.

FURTHER ENCOURAGEMENT

- Read 1 Peter 5:6–11.

- Listen to "Be Not Dismayed" by Mahalia Jackson.

FOR REFLECTION

Have you felt anxiety during this season? Describe it. Journal
about ways God has rescued you in the past and how you see
him doing that in the future.

NOTES

11

Set Your Minds on Things Above

If then you have been raised with Christ,
seek the things that are above, where Christ
is, seated at the right hand of God.
COLOSSIANS 3:1, ESV

WE SCROLL THROUGH our social media feeds, searching Twitter, Facebook, Instagram — for what? We glue our eyes to the news at any and every hour of the day, filling our minds with words and words and words from people we don't know and barely trust. Pandemic panic has set in, and our world is seeking hope and help, but the apostle Paul suggests we may be looking in the wrong places.

Paul reminds us that we have been raised with Christ; that reality changes everything about where we should look for hope and help. He tells us to "seek the things above, where Christ is…" (Colossians 3:1). To seek the things above is to seek the one who first sought us — Jesus. To seek the things above is to look first for the things that Jesus cares most about, his kingdom and his righteousness. As we seek the things above, we find provision for all of our needs, and our anxiety subsides (Matthew 6:25–34).

Not only must we seek the things above, we must "set [our] minds on the things that are above, not on things that are on earth" (Colossians 3:2). We must "set our minds," or "fix our minds." To fix our minds is to have the intense concentration of a world-champion chess player, to have the laser focus of a brain surgeon. To fix our minds is to turn away from our fixation with non-stop news in order to fill our minds with the things of Christ, his rule and his reign, his glory and his grace.

Setting our minds on things above does *not* mean that we ignore the things of this earth. It simply means that we begin by seeking Christ in Scripture, in prayer, and in fellowship with other believers. As we set our compass on Christ, we remain on course to live as he has called us to live on this earth. During crisis, moms and medical people, delivery workers and truck drivers will focus their minds and energy on the earthly tasks that need to be accomplished to care for those they serve. But they will do so while praying, "Your kingdom come, your will be done, on *earth* as it is in heaven" (Matthew 6:10).

Finally, setting our minds on the things above will help us remember that the day of restoration is coming. When our lives are centered on Christ, we are always scanning the horizon, watching for his return, waiting for the day when we will live with him in the new heavens and the new earth. In that day, in that place, we will "appear with him in glory" (Colossians 3:4), living and loving forever in his perfect peace.

Lord Christ,

Draw our eyes away from our screens and toward your glorious presence on the throne next to our heavenly Father. Help us to set our minds on you and seek to live out your love on this earth. In your glorious name. AMEN.

FURTHER ENCOURAGEMENT:

- Read Colossians 3:1–3; Matthew 6:25–34.

- Listen to "Turn Your Eyes upon Jesus" by Lauren Daigle.

FOR REFLECTION

Do you find yourself filling your mind with things of this earth during crisis? Make a list of three ways you could set your mind on things above and schedule times on your calendar to do them.

12

Unspoken

For we do not know how to pray as we
ought, but the Spirit himself intercedes for
us with groanings too deep for words.
ROMANS 8:26, ESV

WHEN OUR SON was diagnosed with a brain tumor, I readily shared prayer requests for our many needs. Even as I shared, it occurred to me that many people do not ask for prayer because their crisis seems too painful or private to share. Maybe their daughter was harming herself, or their son was addicted to drugs, or their husband's business was failing.

If you struggle to find a voice or a place to share your prayer requests, whether because of sorrow or shame or shock, take heart. The good news of the gospel is that your Father knows your needs before you ask, the Holy Spirit and the Son are interceding for you, and God has provided trustworthy people on this earth to pray for you. Let's consider each of these provisions.

First, Jesus, in teaching his disciples to pray simply and secretly, assured them, "your Father knows what you need even before you ask him" (Matthew 6:9). Unlike the robots

Alexa or Siri, God always listens to our hearts and always understands our needs and requests, whether they're spoken or unspoken.

Not only is the Father "attentive to our prayers" (1 Peter 5:12), he has also given us the Holy Spirit to dwell in us and to join us in our "unutterable groanings" (Romans 8:26). As the Spirit groans in us, the Father translates our requests and transforms our hearts, providing for our deepest needs (Romans 8:27).

Not only is the Holy Spirit interceding for us, Jesus himself, the great High Priest sits on a throne beside his Father in heaven, interceding for us. According to Hebrews 7:25, "Therefore he is able, once and forever, to save those who come to God through him. He lives forever to intercede with God on their behalf" (NLT). What we cannot speak for ourselves, Jesus speaks for us.

In addition to his ever-present attention and his Spirit and his Son's intercession, God has given us in-the-flesh warriors, his church, to pray for us. While you may not want to share private or painful prayer requests with the whole church, you can find relief and healing in sharing your needs with one trusted friend, ministry leader, or pastor (James 5:12). The Lord has provided us community in Christ so we don't have to carry the burdens of crisis alone.

Dear friend, when your crisis feels too painful to share, take heart. The Father who knows all of your needs before you ask has provided a powerful army of prayer warriors to come alongside you and do battle for you.

Father,

You know the agony we feel when we can't share the painful realities of our broken stories. Thank you for assuring us that your Son and your Spirit and your church groan alongside us. In Jesus' advocating name we pray. AMEN.

FURTHER ENCOURAGEMENT

- Read Matthew 6:5–8; Romans 8:25–34; Hebrews 7:25; James 5:12.

- Listen to "Arise My Soul, Arise" by Indelible Grace.

FOR REFLECTION

If you have not been able to share your prayer needs during crisis, describe what that has been like. If you have felt free to share your prayer needs, describe what that has been like.

NOTES

13

Prisoners of Hope

*Return to your fortress, you prisoners
of hope; even now I announce that I
will restore twice as much to you.*
ZECHARIAH 9:12, ESV

IN THE WAKE of the multiple losses crisis can bring—jobs
and businesses lost, loved ones removed by distance or death,
long-anticipated joys like graduations and final celebrations
erased from the calendar, it can feel agonizing to hope. It is
tempting to think we are prisoners trapped in a dungeon of
despair. And yet, into our dungeons of despair, our Redeemer
has come, to draw us out, to make us prisoners of hope.

Zechariah, prophet to the Israelites during their return
from captivity, speaks hope during the uncertain season of
rebuilding the temple. He foretells a day when prisoners will
be set free "from the waterless pit" (Zechariah 9:10). Charles
Spurgeon describes the waterless pits of the Ancient Near East,
which were dug to hold prisoners: "The sides were usually
steep and perpendicular—and the prisoner who was dropped
down into such a pit must remain there without any hope of
escape."[8] Maybe you've felt like a prisoner in such a pit, stuck

in a dark dungeon of despair, overwhelmed by your sins or overwhelmed by your circumstances. It is...

- A dark pit, where light cannot penetrate.

- A waterless pit, where no river of life can flow.

- A walled well of a pit, where no handholds exist to help you climb out.

- A lonely pit, where none can reach you, and you cannot reach others.

- A crowded pit, where accusing demons clamor at you, shouting out your shame.

Into this black pit of despair, Christ entered to captivate us by his love and make us prisoners of his hope.

As Pastor Scotty Smith explains, Jesus is "The Prince of Hope" who brings the "Promise of Hope" who paid the "Price of Hope" so we might become "Prisoners of Hope."[9] Zechariah asserts the "promise of hope" as the reason for rejoicing greatly and shouting loudly: "Behold, your king is coming to you..." (Zechariah 9:9). Our Prince of Hope came riding, not on a massive white horse befitting a king, but on a young donkey, a humble ride for a humble ruler. Our Prince of Hope has won our peace, our peace with God, our peace with one another. His rule of peace and hope extends into the deepest pit and beyond the farthest sea. By paying the "price of hope," his own blood, he sealed our hope of forgiveness of sins, our assurance of God's covenantal love. Our Prince of Hope has restored to us the inheritance of the firstborn: the inheritance of his riches.

Because of our Prince of Hope, we have become Prisoners of Hope. Shout aloud in a voice of triumph! Be glad, be glad, be glad! You are no longer a prisoner in the pit of despair. You are a prisoner of hope, a hope that is secure, a hope that will not disappoint.

PRAYER

Lord Jesus,

Thank you for descending into our pit of despair and bringing us out as your prisoners of hope. Help us keep looking to your rescue and redemption for hope in our current struggles and losses. AMEN.

FURTHER ENCOURAGEMENT

- Read Zechariah 9:9–17.

- Listen to "Jesus Shall Reign" by Keith and Kristyn Getty.

FOR REFLECTION

What does it look like to you to be a prisoner of Christ's hope?

14

You Are with Me

*Even though I walk through the valley
of the shadow of death, I will fear no
evil, for you are with me; Your rod
and your staff, they comfort me.*
PSALM 23:4, ESV

TRAVERSING THE ROAD of recovery often feels like walking through the valley of the shadow of death. Each journey is complex and mysterious, of uncertain length, and fraught with unknown fears. And yet, according to David, who journeyed through many dark valleys, we can "fear no evil," because we are not alone. The Lord is closer than whispering distance, guarding and guiding us with his presence.

Imagine you find yourself in a narrow alleyway running between two tall buildings in a dangerous urban area. No streetlights. No building lights. Stark starless night darkness. You can't see the tips of your fingers, much less the end of the alleyway. It's too late to return to the other side, before you saw what you saw, before the surgeon made the cut, before your loved one died. The recovery road has much in common with David's valley of deep darkness.

Notice that David *walks* through this valley of deep darkness; he doesn't run, even though he might be tempted to do so. Running isn't usually an option when you're recovering from disaster. Notice that David walks *through* this deep valley. There is no way around it; there is no turning back. The only way is to go *through* it, to get to the other side. Notice that David is alone in this deep darkness: "Even though *I* walk." Even when we are in healthy community, we can feel isolated in recovery, as if no one else has ever walked this particular shadowland before.

How would it be possible to fear no evil in a place of such "suspense and surmise," in which "the evil of evils is uncertainty"?[10] The answer comes in the pivot point, verse four, "For *you* are with me." Earlier, David told us that the Lord, third person, is his shepherd; now he addresses the Lord directly:

"You are with me." In other words,
You, the King of kings, are with me.
You, the Lion of Judah, are with me.
You, the Crusher of Satan, are with me.

Take heart, dear friends. His light, the light that has overcome the darkness, has flooded this dark valley. The Lord, your Shepherd, who protects and guides you with his staff, is with you.

Lord,

You are our Shepherd. We trust you to guide us, protect us, and secure us in this dark valley of deep uncertainty. Surround us with your love and mercy that we may never stray from you. AMEN.

FURTHER ENCOURAGEMENT

- Read Psalm 23.

- Listen to "God Is My Shepherd" by Jon Foreman.

FOR REFLECTION

What dark valley are you walking through right now? What is uncertain and frightening? How does it help to know the Lord is your shepherd?

NOTES

15

Naked and Unashamed

*And the man and his wife were both
naked and were not ashamed.*
GENESIS 2:25, ESV

ME TOO. MORE than once. By men in authority over me, by men much older than me. Men who took my teenage trust and twisted it for their own wicked purposes. Every sexually charged word, every sexually charged touch, left its mark on me, scarring me with the deep scarlet of shame. Many crises brand us with a scar of shame not of our own making. We hunch over in our nakedness, hoping to hide our glaring defects. Recovery can take a lifetime, if not an eternity.

Recovery requires that we reclaim God's original design of our dignity: "And the man and his wife were both naked and not ashamed" (Genesis 2:25). Into the hunching of our false shame, Scripture calls us to remember our glorious creation: "So God created man in his own image, in the image of God he created him; male and female he created them" (Genesis 1:26–27). He created male and female, each of us with our own unique body, our own unique face. God created us to be his image-bearers, chosen representatives of his kindness and his kingdom.

Although the glory and honor of male and female, God's crown of creation, were marred in the fall, Scripture offers powerful reasons to hope for freedom from shame:

- Jesus, our Savior, the Son of God, was betrayed and beaten, despised and disfigured on our behalf. His very wounds healed us from our shame (Isaiah 53:3–5, 7–12).

- Nailed naked to a tree, Jesus "endured the cross, despising the shame, for the joy set before him" (Hebrews 12:1–3).

- Jesus also clothed himself in the shame of our sin as well as the shame of others' sins against us. In so doing, he covered our nakedness and shame with the bright robe of his righteousness (2 Corinthians 5:21).

- One day, Jesus, our bridegroom, will return. When he does so, he will complete the restoration work on our demeaned dignity. In that day, wearing the luminous wedding dress befitting the bride of Christ, we will be crowned with Christ's glory (Revelation 21:2).

Dear friend, if someone or something has caused you to doubt your loveliness as God's creation, if shame has left its scarlet scar, join me, join Christ, in despising that shame. Look up to the cross, to the One who has redeemed you, and take heart. He is even now recovering and reclaiming you as his own treasured possession.

Father God,

Help us remember that you are our Creator and our Redeemer, our Re-coverer and our Restorer. When we feel the rising rouge of shame brought on by another's abuse, help us see ourselves through your eyes as the restored bride of Christ. Help us to trust in you as our only Savior from others' sins and our own. In Jesus' restoring name. AMEN.

FURTHER ENCOURAGEMENT

- Read Genesis 1:26–27; Isaiah 53:3–5, 7–9; Hebrews 12:1–3.

- Listen to "With Great Gentleness" by Sandra McCracken.

FOR REFLECTION

Have you experienced a sense of shame due to a shattering in your life? Set a timer for twenty minutes and write about this experience. Then set a timer for fifteen minutes and meditate on how Jesus has recovered and restored you. Write about what gives you hope as you see Jesus' redemptive work. Try repeating this exercise four days in a row.

NOTES

16

Never Forsaken

It is the Lord who goes before you. He
will be with you; he will not leave you or
forsake you. Do not fear or be dismayed.
DEUTERONOMY 31:8, ESV

AFTER UNDERGOING THREE shoulder surgeries in a year and a
half, I began to feel a little forsaken. My family, although they
cared well for me, carried on with their normal lives while I
lay on the sofa, too pain-ridden and weary to accompany them
on a park outing. I didn't have the energy to join my friends
at Bible study, and although they checked on me, I still felt
alone. Maybe you feel forsaken by a betraying boss or abandoned by the community you lost when your church split.
Crisis and recovery have a way of making us feel forsaken,
forgotten, abandoned, or alone.

In the midst of your sense of forsakenness stands a God who
swears by his own covenantal love never to leave nor forsake
his people. From the beginning in Genesis, he makes cove-
nants with his people: agreements sealed in his sacrificial love,
promising that he will always be committed to them. Even
after they have disobeyed in the garden, he promises Adam

and Eve to send a Son to destroy Satan (Genesis 3:15). He promises Abraham to make him a great nation (Genesis 12:2). He promises his great nation, the Israelites, to bring them into the Promised Land. He assures them he will go before them, be with them, not leave or forsake them (Deuteronomy 31:8).

The Lord brings his people into the Promised Land, but they repeatedly forsake him, abandoning him for other gods. Because of their rebellion, the Lord allows the Israelites to be taken into captivity in Babylon. But he never forsakes them. The prophet Isaiah brings his message of reassurance to the grieving Israelites, "'For the mountains may depart, and the hills may be removed, but my steadfast love will not depart from you, and my covenant of peace shall not be removed,' says the Lord, who has compassion on you" (Isaiah 54:10). In crisis, you may feel forsaken by friends or family, but you will always have the Lord's steadfast love.

How can this be? Only through our Savior's willingness to be forsaken by his Father. On the cross, Jesus was "pierced for our transgressions...crushed for our iniquities" (Isaiah 53:5). In all the suffering he endured for us, what agonized him most was knowing he would be separated from his Father when he died for our sins. And so he cried from the cross, "My God, my God, why have you forsaken me?" (Matthew 27:46). That cry assures us that we will never be forsaken.

In this season of recovery, you may feel forsaken, forgotten, abandoned, alone, as you never have before. In your loneliness, do not forsake your Father. Instead, lean into his everlasting and covenantal kindness in the Son and through the Spirit, your constant companions in grief.

Father,

Thank you for enveloping us in your everlasting, unchanging love. Thank you for sending your Son so that we might not ever know true forsakenness. In Jesus' name. AMEN.

FURTHER ENCOURAGEMENT

- Read Deuteronomy 31:8; Isaiah 54.

- Listen to "You Are My King" by Chris Tomlin.

FOR REFLECTION

In what ways have you felt forsaken, forgotten, abandoned, or alone? How does knowing God's covenantal love for you encourage you?

NOTES

17

A Safe Place

Be merciful to me, O God, be merciful to
me, For in you my soul takes refuge; In the
shadow of your wings I will take refuge,
Till the storms of destruction pass by.
PSALM 57:1, ESV

WHEN THE STORMS of destruction whip through your life, you may feel like David, hunkered down in a cave, singing dirges to the tune of "Do Not Destroy" (Psalm 57, subtitle). As people, places, and things you once held dear are ripped from your life, what you need, like David, is a safe place. What you need even more, is a safe Person.

David, a man after God's own heart, the future king of Israel, has become the target of King Saul, who envies David and seeks to annihilate him. David describes his persecution: roaring lions stalk his soul; "fiery beasts" prowl nearby when he lies down at night; the tongues and teeth of spears and arrows lash at his heart, soul, mind, and body (Psalm 57:4). If David's description sounds familiar to you, then you know what it's like to feel unsafe and uncertain, to be in dire need of a safe place, a refuge, a place of protection and rest.

David shows us where to turn: "I cry out to God Most High" (Psalm 57:2). Calling on God Most High empowers us in two ways: first, it reminds us that our mighty God always has the victory over our enemy, the evil one; and second, it acts as a weapon against the enemy who might lead us to doubt God's might and mercy. Indeed, God Most High sends his steadfast love from heaven to shame the trampler (Psalm 57:3).

As God Most High sends out his salvation, his glory covers the entire earth, even David, even you (Psalm 57:5). Imagine this weighted blanket of glory covering you, protecting you from your enemies. No net set for your steps, no pit dug for your soul, can trip you up when you are covered by the glory of the Most High. The Most High turns your enemies' designs against them, and they fall into their own pits (Psalm 57:6).

As David calls on God Most High and sees how God responds, his fear is transformed to trust. His woeful song becomes a song of worship (Psalm 57:8). Although he did not know him yet, David sang of the refuge we know now in our perfect safe place, our perfect safe Person — Jesus. In Jesus, we have the ultimate protection and peace: no trap of the enemy, no tongue of the accuser, can separate us from the love of Christ our Savior (Romans 8:31).

Dear friend, sing and make melody with David today. The Lord has sent his Son from heaven to cover you with his glory. You are safe in him.

PRAYER

God Most High,

Awaken our hearts to sing of the safety we know
in Jesus, our refuge. Open our eyes to see him
defeating the enemies that prowl about us; nestle us
in his protective covering. In Jesus' secure name we
ask. AMEN.

FURTHER ENCOURAGEMENT

- Read Psalm 57.

- Listen to "This Is Our God" by Chris Tomlin.

FOR REFLECTION

In what ways have you felt pursued by enemies in this season? How have you seen God send salvation from heaven?

NOTES

18

The Accuser

*Therefore, put on every piece of God's
armor so you will be able to resist
the enemy in the time of evil.*
EPHESIANS 6:13, NLT

HE PROWLS AROUND like a lip-licking lion, drooling when he sniffs the vulnerability and frailty of a crisis victim. He is a liar, a tempter, an accuser, and an adversary. He is the prince of demons and the ruler of darkness. He doesn't wear a red suit, he doesn't have horns, and he's not one bit funny. He is the devil, who seeks to do us harm and to destroy our faith. We can be particularly prone to his attacks during crisis and recovery; however, we have two powerful reasons to hope. First, we are well-protected from his schemes with secret weapon armor provided by the Commander of heaven's military, God himself. Second, Christ has already won the ultimate victory over our wily accuser (Colossians 2:15).

Three of Satan's favorite strategies are deception, distraction, and degradation:

Deception: He may lead us astray by planting doubts about God's goodness, just as he did with Adam and Eve. The evil one wants us to believe that God is not "for us" but against us and will deploy many "strategies and tricks" to convince us of this lie (Ephesians 6:11 NLT).

Distraction: Just as he tried to distract Jesus with earthly pleasures and powers (Matthew 4:1–11), the father of lies will seek to distract us. He launches his fiery darts at our vulnerable spots of pain, stress, and fear. He tempts us to escape our distress by abusing good gifts from God, gifts like food, drink, sex, work, exercise, even Christian service. The devil schemes to distract us from serving and seeking the Lord.

Degradation: The accuser loves to shout our shame over us. His degradation may take the form of beating us up about our own sinful tendencies. In this months-long pandemic quarantine, I have often heard an inward voice accusing, "Why are you being such a jerk? You're a Christian; you shouldn't lose your temper so easily." That accusing voice may be my voice; it may be the voice of Satan. I know one thing. It is not the voice of the Lord Jesus who beckons me to come to him with my sin-weary soul.

How do we resist this evil enemy who seeks to destroy our only hope, the hope of Jesus Christ?

We wrestle his lies to the ground with the strong arm of God's salvation, the lasting truth taught in Scripture, the peace earned for us by Christ's death. We stand firm over the defeated devil, remembering our new status in Christ: righteous, forgiven. If our adversary tries to get back up and go again, we shove him back down with Scripture and stand over him with prayer, empowered by the Holy Spirit. Most of all, we remember that Christ has won the ultimate defeat over our persistent prowler, and we look forward to the day when the cruel tyrant will be tossed into the lake of fire forever (Revelation 20:7–10).

PRAYER

God, Our Commander,

Thank you. You have equipped us to stand against the schemes of our enemy, the father of lies. Strengthen us to resist him that he may flee from us. Help us draw near to you, as you draw near to us. In Jesus' conquering name. AMEN.

FURTHER ENCOURAGEMENT

- Read Ephesians 6:10–18; Revelation 20:7–10.

- Listen to "Power in the Blood" by Ashley Cleveland.

FOR REFLECTION

In what ways do you think the devil may be deceiving, distracting, or degrading you? How can you stand against these schemes?

NOTES

19

Enjoying God

The Lord your God is in your midst, a mighty
one who will save; He will rejoice over you
with gladness; he will quiet you by his love;
he will exult over you with loud singing.
ZEPHANIAH 3:17, ESV

CRISIS OFTEN STEALS our joy and hinders us from fulfilling our primary purpose in life: "to glorify God and to enjoy him forever."[11] The shamed and bereft husband who has been left by an adulterous wife loses his joy. The gifted financial adviser laid off when the economy crashes loses her joy. How do we recover our capacity to enjoy and glorify God? We begin by recognizing his enjoyment and delight in us.

The "lost" son of Luke 15 knew what it was like to lose his joy. Having demanded (and, surprisingly, received) his inheritance from his father and run off to squander it, he landed, literally, in a pigsty. Desperate for food during a famine, he determined that he would return home, ask forgiveness of his father, and beg for a job as a hired hand. He entertained no thought of earning his father's favor back. There was no joy in his heart as he trudged home, only the faint hope of being fed in exchange for his work (Luke 15:11–20).

Imagine, then, the squandering son's shock and delight when his father humiliated himself by running toward his son (unthinkable in that culture). The betrayed father hugged and kissed his son. Before the son could even finish his rehearsed speech, his father had turned away to order the servants to kill the biggest, fattest calf they could find and throw the juicy steaks on the fire. The wildly generous father covered his son with his robe and gave him his ring as a sign of restored relationship. His son had been lost, but now he was found. There would be feasting and celebration in the father's house today (Luke 11:20–24). Jesus tells this parable to demonstrate our Father's extravagant love for us.

What happens when sinners grasp the Lord's delight in them? The Samaritan woman of John 4 runs to invite those she had formerly avoided to come and see Jesus. The "sinful" woman of Luke 7 crashes a feast thrown for Jesus, pouring her tears on his feet, showering him with her love (Luke 7:36–50). When people experience God's lavish love, his undeserved forgiveness, and his full adoption, they cannot contain the good news. They glorify the Lord with their lips and in their lives.

This, dear friends, is how we regain our joy and recover our primary purpose in life. We keep returning to the Father, who has shared his bountiful feast of mercy and grace with us. We hear him sing over us, and we sing out the good news of his quieting love to others. Such is the life of enjoying and glorifying God forever. Preach this good news to your heart and refuse the one who tries to tell you you'll never know joy again.

Lord,

We have lost our joy, and we want it back. Thank you for the feast you have already thrown to celebrate our return. As you delight in us and sing your love over us, we sing out our love and delight in you. In Jesus' name. AMEN.

FURTHER ENCOURAGEMENT

- Read Luke 15:11–32; Psalm 67; Zephaniah 3:14–17.

- Listen to "Rejoice, the Lord Is King" by Emu Music.

FOR REFLECTION

Have you lost some of your joy? How does grasping God's enjoyment of you help you to enjoy and glorify him?

NOTES

20

All Your Needs

My God shall supply every need of yours
according to his riches in glory in Christ Jesus.
PHILIPPIANS 4:19, ESV

WILL THE MONEY run out before the month does? How will I care for my wife who was left a paraplegic by a car accident? Who will father my children now that my husband has abandoned us? Crisis can leave us with a vast and deep chasm of need. Into this chasm, God showers his riches in glory in Christ Jesus. When we meditate on the wealth and power of the God who meets our needs, we discover every reason for hope and peace. Who is this God?

He is the God who birthed the future of his nation from a ninety-year-old woman's barren womb; he is the God who birthed his Son the Savior from the womb of a teenage virgin.

He is the God who made a path of dry land through the sea, rescuing his people from their slave masters; he is the God who defeated your slave masters, Satan and sin, through Christ's death and resurrection.

He is the God who fed his people with manna daily dropped from the sky as they wandered in the wilderness; he is the God who sent Jesus to feed five thousand with five loaves of bread and two fish.

He is the God who aeronautically engineered the powerful wings of an eagle; he is the God who sent his Spirit to give strength to the weary that you may run and not faint.

He is the God who feeds the birds of the air and clothes the lilies of the field; he is the God who sends Jesus, the Best Samaritan, to feed love to the victimized and to clothe the shamed.

He is the God who is the shepherd of his sheep, healing their wooly wounds with oil, leading them by still water; he is the God who sent his Son as your Shepherd, to bind up your broken heart and to lead you to living water.

He is the God who shone the bright light of his Son into his people's darkness; he is the same God who will guide your paths by his Spirit and show you the way through your confusion.

He is the God who forsook his Son on the cross; He is the God who adopted you as his son or daughter through Christ's sacrifice for you.

He is the God who numbers the hairs on your head, counts your tears, and saves them in a bottle; he is the God who will one day wipe away all tears.

In this season, it may be tempting to stare hopelessly into the dark and vast hole of need that the explosion of crisis has left in your home, health, or heart. Focus instead on the provision of your rich and glorious God, your generous Father, who has given you all things in Christ. Trust your cares to the one who cares for you. He will supply all your needs with his immeasurable riches.

Father God,

We are needy. We don't just need help — we need you. Thank you for your abundant grace; help us to live in hope because of your provision. In Jesus' glorious name. AMEN.

FURTHER ENCOURAGEMENT

- Read Philippians 4:4–19; Ephesians 3:14–21.
- Listen to "I Need Thee Every Hour" by Heather Headley.

FOR REFLECTION

Which of the above realities about God gives you hope in the face of your current needs?

NOTES

21

Pray about Everything

Don't worry about anything; instead, pray
about everything. Tell God what you need,
and thank him for all he has done.
PHILIPPIANS 4:6, NLT

YEARS AGO, OUR Gulf coast city narrowly averted disaster when a hurricane heading our way shifted at the last minute. Afterwards, a fellow soccer mom told me how she had dealt with her worry. Fearing that their seventy-year-old home wouldn't hold up in the storm, she said, "We stayed inside and thought happy thoughts."

There's nothing wrong with happy thoughts, but they are a poor antidote for the toxin of worry injected by crisis. In Philippians, the apostle Paul tells of a much more potent remedy to the worry and fear presented by crisis—prayer. In Philippians 4:4–9, we discover a three-fold process of prayer which allays fears in the direst of circumstances.

Paul calls us to begin our defense against worry with a prayer of rejoicing (Philippians 4:4). Rejoicing in the Lord defuses worry by re-orienting our hearts and minds to what matters most in life—the Lord's enjoyment of us, which we have in

Christ; and our enjoyment of him, which is our chief calling as Christians. When we realize our most precious treasure is not our roof, our marriage, our kids, or our mortgage, the devastations of disaster pose little threat. When our most prized possession is our relationship with the Lord, we can truly rejoice, for no one can separate us from him (Romans 8:38).

Paul calls us to continue our prayer defense by presenting our requests to the Lord. As we do so, we acknowledge our lowliness, our utter dependence on our heavenly Father, the King of the cosmos. We approach our Father's throne room with confidence, for Jesus, who gave his life for us, intercedes for us (Romans 8:34). Furthermore, we are hopeful in presenting our requests, because we know that our heavenly Father gives good gifts to his children.

Finally, Paul tells us to pray with thanksgiving. How does thanking God combat worry? As we thank God for how he has saved in the past, our hope for the future is restored. Thanking God also helps us beat down the "why" questions that pop up in crisis like monsters in a carnival game, because it reminds us that God always rules wisely and well. As we give thanks, we regain the peace that comes from trusting God with every detail of our lives.

When storms threaten to shatter our hopes and dreams, we can do better than "thinking happy thoughts." Let's rejoice in the Lord who delights in us, thanking him for all of his goodness, and telling him all of our needs. He will surely answer.

PRAYER

Good, Good Father,

You are our joy and our delight. We thank you for saving us — from our sins, and from utter ruin and disaster. We thank you for being a Father who wants to hear our needs, our fears, our worries. In Jesus' name. AMEN.

FURTHER ENCOURAGEMENT

- Read Philippians 4:4–7.

- Listen to "Sweet Hour of Prayer" by Casting Crowns.

FOR REFLECTION

What worries and fears are troubling you? Try writing a prayer with three parts: 1. Name a reason you have joy in the Lord 2. Tell God what you need 3. Thank God for what he has already done.

22

Surpassing Peace

And the peace of God, which surpasses
all understanding, will guard your hearts
and your minds in Christ Jesus.
PHILIPPIANS 4:7, ESV

IT SEEMED AN improbable peace, a peculiar peace. It came over me like a protective cloak, easing my mind and my body. The occasion was our son's first brain surgery after a tumor had been discovered. In these terrifying hours, the peace I experienced truly surpassed all understanding.

As we combat the worry that crops up in crisis with the rejoicing, gentleness, prayer, and thanksgiving described in Philippians 4:4–7, we discover the peace of God. This peace proves more powerful than a tank brigade in protecting our hearts and minds from worry. Let's look at seven ways it does so.

First, it is the peace of God. The peace belongs to God, and it characterizes God. Can you imagine God wringing his hands, fretting over the what-if's that worry us? I can't. That's because he is the God of peace and order. That's because he is the all-powerful and all-knowing ruler of the universe.

Second, it is a surpassing peace. It is far lovelier than the silence that descends when sugar-charged children have finally fallen asleep on Christmas Eve. It is far more calming than the soothing scent of a lavender candle. It is far more enduring than a two-fingered peace sign flashed to a friend.

Third, this peace surpasses all understanding. It blows our minds and stirs our hearts. It is a puzzling peace, a seemingly impossible peace given the situation. It is the kind of peace that makes people say, "I can't explain how I felt so calm in the midst of that crisis."

Fourth, it is a peace that guards our hearts and guards our minds. It is our own personal bodyguard blocking the path of any doubts, worries, fears, or complaints that would attempt attack.

Fifth, it is a peace that comes from being "in Christ Jesus." It is the stable peace of knowing our foundation is sure. It is the secure peace of knowing the perfecting love of our heavenly Father. It is the saving peace of knowing nothing can destroy us. It is the peace of Christ.

Sixth, it is a peace that focuses us on the God of peace. It is a peace that leads us to fix our minds on the true, the just, the lovely—all of the things of God that are "worthy of praise" (Philippians 4:8). With such thoughts filling our minds, peace abounds even more.

Finally, and most importantly, it is a peace that reminds us that the God of peace is with us (Philippians 4:9). Not only has the God of peace come near in Christ, bringing us lasting peace, the God of peace remains in us through his Holy Spirit.

Dear friends, whatever fears, doubts, or worries your current crisis presents, find your rest in the peace of God and the God of peace. He is with you.

PRAYER

God of Peace,

Your surpassing peace calms our frantic thoughts, rests our worried souls. Thank you for protecting our hearts and minds with the supreme bodyguard, the powerful peace of Christ. In his strong name we pray. AMEN.

FURTHER ENCOURAGEMENT

- Read Philippians 4:4–9.

- Listen to "Find You Here" by Ellie Holcomb.

FOR REFLECTION

What aspects of the peace of God have you known in this season?

NOTES

(23)

Call Me Bitter

*Call me Mara, for the Almighty has
made life very bitter for me.*
RUTH 1:20, NLT

FIRST, A FAMINE sent her small family into exile in a foreign
land. Then her husband died. Then her two sons married
unbelieving women. Then her two sons died. Naomi knew
something about profound loss. And she wasn't so sure recovery
was possible.

In her bottomless grief, Naomi turned sour. When she and her
daughter-in-law returned to Bethlehem, her appearance was so
darkened by disaster that the women of the town asked, "Is it
really Naomi?" (Ruth 1:19 NLT). The Hebrew makes a play on
words: Naomi's name means "pleasant"—we can imagine the
women gesturing toward Naomi, asking, "Is *this* 'pleasant'?"

Indeed, Naomi was the antithesis of pleasant at this moment,
and she wasn't shy about saying so: "Do not call me Naomi; call
me Mara, for the Almighty has dealt very bitterly with me. I
went away full, and the Lord has brought me back empty. Why
call me Naomi, when the Lord has testified against me and the

Almighty has brought calamity upon me?" (Ruth 1:20–21). "Mara" means bitter. Naomi says flatly, "Call me bitter."

Naomi's bitterness was caused by temporary faith amnesia: she had forgotten the Israelites' story of wilderness redemption; she had forgotten God's transformation of the bitter waters at Marah (Exodus 15:23–26). Naomi's bitterness was also caused by temporary hope amnesia; she had forgotten to look for redemption in the midst of loss. Bitterness can lead to blindness, causing us to miss God's provision in our painful circumstances.

The good news of the gospel is that the Lord does not condemn us for our gospel amnesia. The Lord never forgets to be faithful; the Lord never forgets to restore our hope; the Lord always remembers to love us. The Lord redeems and restores even when we are at our worst. Naomi's hope was gradually awakened, first by Boaz's kindness to Ruth in the field (Ruth 2:20) and then by the blessing of a grandchild (Ruth 4:13). By the end of the story, the same women who couldn't reconcile Naomi's appearance with the name "pleasant" were celebrating the reason for her renewed hope: "Praise the Lord, who has now provided a redeemer for you and your family! May he restore your youth and care for you in your old age" (Ruth 4:14–15 NLT). Indeed, Naomi's grandchild, Obed, was the grandfather of King David and an ancestor of King Jesus, the ultimate restorer of youth.

Dear friends, when the darkness closes in and your heart turns sour, look back, look up, look around. The Lord has redeemed and will redeem again. Never make the mistake of thinking the story is over until it's over. You'll know when it's over, because final restoration will be so very sweet.

PRAYER

Lord, Almighty,

You give and you take away. Forgive our amnesia, forgive us for forgetting the mighty works you've done in the past. Forgive our stubbornness, our refusal to look for your provision in the present. Soften and sweeten our hearts when they become bitter because of loss. In Jesus' redeeming name we pray. AMEN.

FURTHER ENCOURAGEMENT

- Read Ruth 1–4.

- Listen to "Fool's Gold" by Sandra McCracken.

FOR REFLECTION

Have you felt bitter or angry toward God in your grief? Write a prayer telling God what's on your mind. Ask him to reveal his redemptive work in your life.

NOTES

24

Courage for Crisis

Wherever you go, I will go; wherever you live, I will live. Your people will be my people, and your God will be my God.
RUTH 1:16, NLT

RUTH HAD NO good reason to follow Naomi. When Naomi decided to return to Bethlehem from Moab, she released her two daughters-in-law, telling them she had no hope to offer them. Orpah departed. Ruth remained. Why?

Ruth's profound proclamation of commitment to Naomi gives us a clue, "your God will be my God" (Ruth 1:16 NLT). Ruth was raised in Moab, where people worshiped many pagan gods. But there was something that drew her to sojourn in the land of her deceased husband's God. She might not have known it yet, but she would know it soon: God, by his grace, had planted a seed of faith in Ruth that would grow into redemption for many people.

Ruth's willingness to risk traveling into unfamiliar territory reminds us of the heroes of faith described in Hebrews 11. Faith bolsters courage to venture into the unknown, even, or especially, in seasons of crisis. By God's grace, through faith, Ruth courageously moved into many unknown places:

- She traveled to Bethlehem, a land she didn't know, with a hope that wasn't assured (Ruth 2:16).

- She stooped to glean in the field of a stranger, making herself vulnerable to assault, trusting that God would provide sustenance for her and Naomi (Ruth 2:2–18).

- She lay on the threshing-floor of Boaz, going along with her mother-in-law's strange plot to procure a husband. (Ruth 3:1–5).

- She reached far beyond Naomi's plan to actually propose marriage to Boaz (Ruth 3:8–9).

Make no mistake, Ruth's actions were risky, extremely unconventional, in her culture. Her courage came from her simple but sound faith; her faith likely came from her remembrance of redemption stories Naomi's family had told. She trusted this redeeming God, believing he would redeem again. And he did.

Ruth's courage compels us to ask, "How will we face crisis and loss?" Will it be with the courage of faith? Will we keep taking steps into unknown, unfamiliar territory, trusting that the Lord Almighty is at work, orchestrating redemption and renewal? We have far more reason than Ruth to risk action. Ruth's kinsman-redeemer was a man; our Kinsman-Redeemer is Jesus. Boaz paid a price, a sum of money, to redeem Ruth. Jesus paid a higher price, the sum of his life — death, to redeem us. Yes, we have reason to risk, the courage of faith to move into crisis with humility and hope, with love and loyalty. God, by his grace, has grown this seed of faith in us. Let us bear the fruit.

PRAYER

Our Mighty God,

We come to you, seeking the courage of faith that only you can give us. Strengthen us to go to the unfamiliar places, to love in unfamiliar ways. Help us to trust that you are writing your love story in our lives through our Bridegroom. AMEN.

FURTHER ENCOURAGEMENT

- Read Ruth 1–4.

- Listen to "Lead On, O King Eternal" by Sara Groves.

FOR REFLECTION

What actions do you need to take that will require the courage of faith? List two-three here, and write a date by which you will have completed them. Then ask God to give you the faith you need.

NOTES

25

The Sleep of the Beloved

*It is in vain that you rise up early and go
late to rest, eating the bread of anxious
toil; for he gives to his beloved sleep.*
PSALM 127:2, ESV

THE TOSSING AND turning of insomnia may insinuate itself along with crisis, leaving us longing for rest. My insomnia began when I was twelve and has never really given way to easy sleep. After a bicycle crash in which I shattered my elbow in twenty-five-ish places, I was placed in traction for three weeks and given narcotics to ease the pain. During this same season, a school friend died in a freak accident. Once I was released from the hospital, still wearing a cast on my arm, sleep stubbornly refused to come. Night after night, I lay awake, following the shadows cast by lights from a nearby convenience store, aroused by the noises of people coming and going.

Many nights I've passed since then, awake, praying, begging God to help me fall asleep. I must confess, in the weak moments of shadowy nights, I've occasionally wondered, "Does it mean that I am not one of his beloved, since he does not give me sleep?" I must also confess, though, that the Lord has never let me go an entire night without sleep.

What God does give, and what Psalm 127 invites us to, is rest. Not only does he give it; he commands it (Exodus 20:8–11), because we need it. When we have suffered from danger and trauma, we need more than ever to heed the Lord's invitation to rest. In seasons of recovery, we can become anxious and hyper-vigilant as we strive to restore order. The Psalms remind us of our reason to rest—our God is a mighty guard watching over us and keeping us:

The Lord who built the house (and created us) watches over the city and its people—us (Psalm 127:1). The Lord is our "keeper," (Psalm 121:5), that is, someone who "exercise(s) great care over."[12] He keeps us from "all evil," keeps "our life," and keeps our "going out and our coming in" (Psalm 121:7–8). He keeps us "from this time forth and forevermore." And even when we can't sleep, we have good company: "Behold, he who keeps Israel will neither slumber nor sleep" (Psalm 127:4).

One day, our anxious toil will give way to the full rest of restoration: "We shall not all sleep, but we shall all be changed in a moment, in the twinkling of an eye, at the last trumpet" (1 Corinthians 15:52). As for me, I don't know if there will be sleep in heaven, but I like to think so. I do know—in that day, the Father who keeps me will grant me rest even sweeter than the deepest sleep.

PRAYER

Lord, our Creator and Keeper,

Thank you for watching over us, for relieving us of any reason for anxiety. Help those of us who struggle to sleep; show us your watchful and protective presence. Most of all, help us to rest and trust in your kind and strong keeping. AMEN.

FURTHER ENCOURAGEMENT

- Read Psalms 121:1–8; 127:1–5; 131.

- Listen to "Sleepless Night" by Fernando Ortega.

FOR REFLECTION

When you struggle to sleep or rest, how does it help to know that the Lord is watching and keeping you?

NOTES

26

Waiting with Hope

We too, wait with eager hope for the day
when God will give us our full rights
as his adopted children, including the
new bodies he has promised us.
ROMANS 8:23B, ESV

Waiting for hours to buy gas after a hurricane.

Waiting for weeks for workmen's compensation to
authorize a surgery.

Waiting for months to recover from a heart attack.

Waiting for years to have one happy day after the death
of a child.

WHENEVER OUR STORIES are shattered by crisis, a season of waiting will likely follow. Waiting can be irritating at a long pharmacy drive-thru line, but in the profound losses of a crisis, it can be agonizing. What does it look like to wait with hope as we grieve our losses?

First we must recognize the difference between earthly hope and biblical hope. Earthly hope focuses on good outcomes in the here and now, or at least the near future. There is nothing wrong with such hope—hoping that the surgery is approved and that the recovery goes smoothly, hoping that the betrayal will sting less tomorrow than it does today. And yet, earthly hope is often limited by our own short-sightedness, our inability to see everything our all-seeing God sees. To all earthly hope, we need to add biblical hope.

Biblical hope, as defined by Dan Allender and Tremper Longman is a "vision of redemption in the midst of decay."[13] Biblical hope is based on faith, on remembering how God has rescued in the past: "Now faith is the assurance of things hoped for, the conviction of things not seen" (Hebrews 11:1 ESV). Biblical hope focuses on the end of the story, the day when Jesus will return and restore all broken things (Romans 8:18–19). In that day, we will be restored to our Father as his adopted children, and all of creation's groaning will end in fruitful labor, Christ's perfected new creation (2 Corinthians 5:17).

When we wait with biblical hope, we will continue to pray for God's good gifts on this earth: gas to fuel generators after a hurricane, a sweet memory on a loved one's death day. Biblical hope leads us to pray, "God, if I don't get the gas today, help me be patient and trust your provision," or "If I am sad all day long, be near to me in my grief." When our earthly hopes are disappointed, biblical hope compels us to look and lean toward the final day when "all things work together for good" in the lives of those who trust God for life and salvation (Romans 8:28).

Dear friends, when the wait feels excruciating, remember that you have evidence that your deepest hopes will not go unfulfilled: Christ has already come to rescue and redeem. Remember what you are waiting for—glory itself! Knowing this, keep hoping with an active imagination, leaning into the future, leaning into God's loving purposes in our hardest waits.

PRAYER

Lord,

How long? This is our cry as we wait in impossibly long lines or for seemingly improbable recoveries. Draw our eyes to the horizon, to see Jesus "coming soon" to end our grievous wait. In Jesus' already-redeeming name. AMEN.

FURTHER ENCOURAGEMENT

- Read Romans 8:18–30.

- Listen to "Spring Is Coming" by Steven Curtis Chapman.

FOR REFLECTION

How has waiting felt for you in this crisis? How have you been disappointed in earthly hopes? How might remembering the end of the biblical Story help you wait with patience?

NOTES

27

Give Thanks in All Circumstances?

Give thanks in all circumstances.
1 THESSALONIANS 5:18, ESV

IS THAT REALLY possible? To "give thanks in all circumstances"? As author Ann Voskamp asks, "How do I see grace, give thanks, find joy in this sin-stinking place?"[14] When we suffer profound loss, it can seem impossible to give thanks. And yet, the apostle Paul believes we not only can but we must.

It's not as if the apostle Paul was sitting on silky sand drinking a piña colada when he wrote these words. The apostle Paul suffered imprisonments, shipwreck, beatings, betrayal, poverty, and mockery, among other miseries. In 2 Corinthians 4, Paul describes a cycle of glory, grief, grace, gratitude and glory. This cycle is what compels him to give thanks, even in dire circumstances.

Paul first explains what God has already done: revealed his glory in Christ. When Christ suffered on the cross, he aroused our hearts, enabling us to see the glory of God shining in the darkness (2 Corinthians 4:6). Because his light now shines in our hearts, our response to crisis is transformed. We are…

Squeezed but not squashed

Bewildered but not befuddled

Pursued but not abandoned

Knocked down but not knocked out…[15] (2 Corinthians 4:8–9).

Notice that Paul neither ignores his suffering nor minimizes it. He names the severity: he felt squeezed, bewildered, pursued, knocked down. And yet, he sees hope in the midst of his suffering, because he sees how other people are being affected. Other people are coming to know God's grace, and because they are, they are giving thanks to God: "And as God's grace reaches more and more people, there will be great thanksgiving…." And as more and more people give thanks to God, more and more people give glory to God (2 Corinthians 4:15 NLT).

Paul thanks God even in the midst of grief because he sees God multiplying the good news in the hearts of many. Paul can also thank God in the midst of grief because he looks toward the as-yet-unseen day when we will be wholly restored: "So we do not lose heart. Though our outer self is wasting away, our inner self is being renewed day by day" (2 Corinthians 4:16 NLT). Paul sees not only his body wasting away, but his sinful self being deconstructed, while his inner self is being reconstructed in the image of Christ.[16] And for that, he is also profoundly grateful.

In the stress, the confusion, even the agony of current crisis, keep thanking God. Thank him for the glory he has already revealed to you in Christ, for his revelation of that glory to others, and for the weight of the glory to come. As Paul tells us, that glory will far outweigh "these light and momentary troubles" (2 Corinthians 4:17).

PRAYER:

Glorious God,

Thank you for revealing your glory to us. Help us to see the light of Christ shining in the darkness of disaster. Multiply gratitude in our hearts and in the hearts of others in this season. In Jesus' glorious name. AMEN.

FURTHER ENCOURAGEMENT

Listen to "10,000 Reasons" by Matt Redman.

FOR REFLECTION

Make a list of things you are grateful for today. Consider keeping a gratitude journal for a week or a month.

NOTES

28

Joy Comes

Weeping may tarry for the night, but
joy comes with the morning.
PSALM 30:5, ESV

TEARS BEGAN SLIPPING out even as I left the doctor's office. I let them flow fully once I was safely inside my car. Tears of sorrow for what I had not known was possible in the past two years. Tears of joy for what I had gained in a fifteen-minute procedure. Tears of wonder — is this really how other people walk around? Without pain gnawing at their hips with every stride?

Because of joint hypermobility and an unspecified connective tissue disorder, my joints often feel like they're being seared in a hot frying pan. When the pain gets intolerable, I seek treatment. The morning of my tears, I had received cortisone injections in both hips. The lidocaine filled the joint space, yielding a pause in pain, a sweet and satisfying temporary relief. I had been limping for around two years.

When we encounter David in Psalm 30, he has also discovered relief, relief from God's anger at his sin, rescue from the mockery of foes, restoration of health, and resuscitation from the "pit of death" (Psalm 30:1–5 NLT). Now, he rejoices and invites us to join him, "Sing praises to the Lord, O you his saints, and give thanks to his holy name.... For his anger is for a moment, and his favor is for a lifetime" (Psalm 30:5).

David remembers his agony; he remembers his foolish season of self-sufficiency; he sees how he discovered the Lord's strength in his own weakness (Psalm 30:6–7). David thanks God for the temporary relief he has known, but he persists in seeking a more permanent restoration of his joy, "To you, O Lord, I cry, and to the Lord I plead for mercy; What profit is there in my death, if I go down to the pit?" (Psalm 30:8–9).

David understands that seasons of joy and seasons of pain may come, but if he trusts in the faithfulness of the Lord, he will know joy continually. It is this certainty that has turned David's mourning into dancing, this certainty that has clothed him with gladness.

This same certainty will cover us in peace and hope: God has already cast off the burden of our deepest pains, that of our sin, placing it on the back of his Son. One day, he will relieve us of our earthly limp forever. In that day, we will dance in glory, we will sing in joy, we will shout our praise.

PRAYER

Dear Lord,

We thank you for sweet relief, for moments, days, and seasons when the dark clouds of pain give way to your warm rays of comfort. Help us to dance in this joy and sing praise unto you forever. AMEN.

FURTHER ENCOURAGEMENT

- Read Psalm 30.

- Listen to "Joyful, Joyful, We Adore Thee" by Page CXVI.

FOR REFLECTION

When have you felt relief from pain on your journey? What brought that relief? Thank God for those moments.

29

When You Despair of Life Itself

For we were so utterly burdened beyond our
strength that we despaired of life itself.
2 CORINTHIANS 1:8, ESV

WE HAVE JUST been told that the COVID-19 death toll in America may be in the hundreds of thousands. It is no exaggeration to say that many people are "despairing of life itself" right now. The apostle Paul did not exaggerate when he claimed to be so overwhelmed beyond his ability to endure that he didn't think he would live through it. We can relate.

Paul catalogues his sufferings in a remarkable list in 2 Corinthians 11:24–29. Opponents were accusing Paul of being a false apostle, arguing that no true apostle would suffer as much as Paul did. Paul retorted that his sufferings made him even more qualified to be an apostle. Consider a brief excerpt from his catalogue:

"In danger from robbers, danger from my own people, danger from Gentiles, danger in the city, danger in the wilderness, danger at sea, danger from false brothers; in toil and hardship, through many a sleepless night, in hunger and thirst, often without food, in cold, and exposure" (2 Corinthians

11:26–27). There is little Paul did not suffer for the sake of the gospel. How does Paul's suffering encourage us when we "despair of life itself"?

First, we should not be surprised when we are overwhelmed, crushed, squeezed, perplexed (2 Corinthians 4:8–9). As Peter says, "Dear friends, don't be surprised at the fiery trials you are going through…" (1 Peter 4:12). In this life, we will have trouble, but we can "be of good cheer," because Christ has "overcome the world" (John 16:33 NKJV).

Second, we should not think we are out of God's will when we are bombarded by suffering. God uses suffering to equip and strengthen us, as he did Paul, for gospel ministry (Romans 5:3–5). As we traverse a blizzard of suffering, the Spirit digs fresh paths for our souls, teaching us not to rely on our own strength but on the strength of "the God who raises the dead" (2 Corinthians 1:9).

Third, we can remember that when we are so overwhelmed by suffering we think we're not going to make it, we are in excellent company. Paul, too, felt this way. And Jesus sweated blood in his agony, asking his Father if the cup of suffering could pass from him (Matthew 26:39).

Finally, even as we suffer blow upon blow, we can turn to our Savior, celebrating his grace, remembering that God has not only saved us but will save others through our suffering (2 Corinthians 4:15). We continue to plead with God for help, asking, seeking, knocking, for the removal of our suffering, as Paul asked for relief from his thorn in the flesh (2 Corinthians 12:8). At the same time, we continue to pray as Jesus taught us: "Your kingdom come; your will be done" (Matthew 6:9–10).

Dear friends, take heart. Even as we may "despair of life itself," we are learning with Paul what it means to be "content with weaknesses, insults, hardships, persecutions, and calamities" (2 Corinthians 12:10).

PRAYER

Lord, we are overwhelmed, but we do not despair. Turn our eyes on Jesus, who is working in this crisis to heal and restore his kingdom. In Jesus' suffering name. AMEN.

FURTHER ENCOURAGEMENT

- Read 2 Corinthians 11:24–29.

- Listen to "God of All Comfort" by Ellie Holcomb.

FOR REFLECTION

Write a letter to God about how you have been overwhelmed, crushed, or despairing in your suffering. Ask him to bring his hope into that hard place.

NOTES

30

Christ's Power for Your Weakness

*Therefore I will boast all the more
gladly of my weaknesses, so that the
power of Christ may rest upon me.*
2 CORINTHIANS 12:9, ESV

THE TWENTY-SOMETHING ATHLETE next to me at PT grunted and groaned as she struggled to lift the five-pound weight with her legs. I glanced at her. Her upper body displayed the strength she had gained as a college tennis player. Her left leg was still striped with strong musculature. But her right leg, which had been braced for two months after surgery for an Achilles tendon rupture, was scrawny and weak. Like the college tennis player, we will experience previously unimagined degrees of weakness when we are recovering from a crisis. The good news of the gospel is that in our weakness we discover our greatest strength: Christ's power and grace are sufficient for all of our needs.

To demonstrate this counterintuitive principle, Paul shares how he was met by God in his weakness. First, he explains, "For we were so utterly burdened beyond our strength that we despaired of life itself" (2 Corinthians 1:8). In that place of weakness, he learned the strength of relying not on himself but on the "God who raises the dead," the God who "delivered us from such a deadly peril" and who, Paul knew, would continue to deliver him (2 Corinthians 1:8–10).

Later in the letter, Paul shares how Jesus joined him in his weakness. Paul suffered from an unspecified ailment, which he describes as a "thorn in the flesh," "a messenger of Satan to harass me" (2 Corinthians 12:7). Paul asked Jesus repeatedly to remove it, but Jesus denied him, saying, "My grace is sufficient for you, for my power is made perfect in weakness" (2 Corinthians 12:9). And that is why Paul boasts of his weakness.

Paul returns to the theme one more time before closing his letter to the Corinthians. This time, he connects knowledge of weakness with restoration: "For we are glad when we are weak and you are strong. Your restoration is what we pray for" (2 Corinthians 13:9). Here, the word "restoration" means being built up inwardly, becoming more mature. Paul understood that as we embrace our weakness, we become more fully who God designed us to be. As we discover God's bountiful provision for our weakness, our faith grows strong, and the body of Christ is built up. This is what it means to "aim for restoration" (2 Corinthians 13:11).

Crisis and recovery offer us the opportunity to experience God's surpassing strength for our profound weakness. Let's embrace our weakness, for through it, Christ's image is being restored in us.

PRAYER

Lord,

We confess, we're not crazy about being weak. Most people brag about their strength. Help us to boast in our weakness, realizing it leads us to rely on you, the God who raises the dead. Even as we face our fragility, grow our desire for Christ's strength in us. AMEN.

FURTHER ENCOURAGEMENT

- Read 2 Corinthians 12:1–10; 2 Corinthians 13:9–11.

- Listen to "How Firm a Foundation" by Wendell Kimbrough.

FOR REFLECTION

What weakness are you struggling with? How is your weakness leading you to rely on God? How are you discovering Christ's grace to be sufficient for this season?

NOTES

(31)

Two Crucial Questions

Where have you come from,
and where are you going?
GENESIS 16:8, ESV

WHEN A MASSIVE wildfire has left us homeless, or an abusive boyfriend has left us loveless, when a co-worker's betrayal has left us jobless, or a child's unplanned pregnancy has left us speechless, we may feel like running away from our disastrous circumstances. If we run, we may end up in a wilderness, lonely and lost. The good news of the gospel is that Jesus himself meets us in that desolate place.

Hagar knew the desperation of disastrous circumstances. Her mistress, Sarai, unable to conceive, decided to use a method common in her culture to produce an heir — she would give her maidservant to her husband. When Sarai's plan worked and Hagar conceived, Hagar became proud and showed contempt to Sarai (Genesis 16:4). Sarai, in turn, "dealt harshly" with Hagar (Genesis 16:6), and Hagar fled — back to Egypt. During her flight, by a spring in the wilderness, Hagar was found by the angel of the Lord (Genesis 16:7).

Hagar's story reminds us of how the angel of the Lord, or Jesus himself, meets us in our desperate flight from disastrous circumstances:

- He finds us. He finds us because he hears our affliction, and he seeks us in our distress (Genesis 16:11, 13). He is the "God-who-sees," the Jesus who is looking for us.

- When he finds us, he treats us with grace and favor. The Lord may ask us two crucial questions which re-awaken our hearts to his kindness:

  ○ "Where have you come from?" (Genesis 16:8). This question re-orients us, asking us to remember how God has previously redeemed and rescued us.

  ○ "Where are you going" (Genesis 16:8)? Like Hagar, we often take off without considering where we are going, and we may end up in a land of sin and unbelief. The question "Where are you going?" draws us to hope, to imagine how God will restore in the midst of disaster.

- The Lord calls us to return. Just as the angel of the Lord gave Hagar a hard command—to return home (where despite how we might see it, she would be provided for and even blessed), he calls us to come home to him and surrender to his plan and provision for our lives.

- He makes a promise of fruitfulness. To Hagar, the angel of the Lord promises that he will multiply her offspring. To us, the Lord makes the same promise: as we return to him, he will continue to grow us, to mature us, and to multiply his kingdom through us. Indeed, through his work in us, he will restore others to himself.

Dear friends, if you are fed up and feel like fleeing, pause for a moment and listen to the One who has already heard your cries. Return to him, and submit to him, and wait to see the story of restoration he will write through your disaster.

PRAYER

Lord, Jesus,

Thank you for listening to our cries and for coming to find us. Help us to return to you and trust in you, even when we can't see what you are doing. In your preserving name. AMEN.

FURTHER ENCOURAGEMENT

- Read Genesis 16.

- Listen to "Who Is like Our God?" by Laura Story.

FOR REFLECTION

Spend fifteen minutes journaling about the two crucial questions, "Where have you come from" and "Where are you going?"

NOTES

32

Though He Slay Me

Though he slay me, yet will I hope in him.
JOB 13:15, ESV

TO TRUST GOD in the midst of one major life-altering event can feel like leaping from stone to stone while crossing a swollen creek; to trust God in the midst of multiple losses can feel like trying to leap over a vast canyon. And yet, Job, a man who experienced multiple catastrophic losses, manages to leap over such a canyon, insisting in the midst of disaster that he will continue to trust God. How do we discover such a persistent faith in the midst of crisis? Let's consider Job's story.

Job's losses are set in motion by a conversation unknown to Job. God calls Satan's attention to Job's uprightness (Job 1:8). Satan argues that if Job lost everything, he would curse God and die (Job 1:9–11). God grants Satan permission to afflict Job, and by the end of Chapter 1, Job's livelihood is lost, and his children have died. By the end of Chapter 2, Job is struck with a disease that covers his body with weeping sores. His wife herself suggests that he curse God and die (Job 2:9), and his friends quickly turn on him.

For the next thirty-something chapters, Job cries out, Job complains, but he does not curse God. Even in the midst of his ranting and raving, Job reveals a deep undergirding of faith. When he learns that his children have died, he declares, "The Lord gave, and the Lord has taken away; blessed be the name of the Lord" (Job 1:21). When his wife suggests that he curse God and die, he refuses (Job 2:10). Even as his complaint continues, Job announces his determination to trust in the Lord, "Though he slay me, I will hope in him" (Job 13:15). His belief in a living Redeemer centers his faith: "For I know that my Redeemer lives, and at the last he will stand upon the earth" (Job 19:25).

Job's loud lament makes many Christians uncomfortable, but the Lord is not unnerved by it. When he eventually meets Job, he unfurls his majesty before him, granting him a macrocosmic display of his powerful presence. The Lord neither deigns to defend himself, nor does he explain Job's suffering; rather he offers Job a sweeter gift, the surety that the Lord is ever-present in his pain. When the Lord wraps up his response, Job professes an even deeper knowledge of the Lord, "I had heard of you by the hearing of the ear, but now my eye sees you" (Job 42:5).

As we remember Job's story, we too are reassured that we can trust the Lord who controls the cosmos with our complaint. Indeed, this same Lord allowed our Redeemer, his own Son, to endure multiple losses which culminated in Christ's death on the cross and his descent to hell. But the story did not end there. Because God raised Jesus from the dead, because our Redeemer lives, we can affirm with Job, "Though he slay me, yet will I hope in him" (Job 13:15).

PRAYER

All-knowing and Ever-present God,

Give us the faith of Job to cry out to you and
to discover you as the loving and majestic God
who is always trustworthy in our suffering. In our
Redeemer's living name. AMEN.

FURTHER ENCOURAGEMENT

- Read the book of Job.

- Listen to "Blessed Be Your Name" by Matt Redman.

FOR REFLECTION

Write a letter to God naming your suffering. Then, reading
Job 38–42, imagine how God might respond to you.

NOTES

33

The Good News of Not Being Fine

Two people are better off than one, for they
can help each other succeed. If one person
falls, the other can reach out and help. But
someone who falls alone is in real trouble.
ECCLESIASTES 4:9, NLT

I GUESS I could blame it on my daughter. She put the idea in my head. It all started when I texted my two girls, asking them to pray because I was going to the doctor to have twenty-five staples removed from my hip. Both agreed to pray, and my younger daughter, who, as a counselor, knows the best methods for dealing with pain and stress, reminded me to take something to squeeze. Good idea, I thought.

There was just one problem. I didn't have one of those squishy de-stresser balls. But now I was committed to squeezing, so I decided to make one. Searching my pantry for something soft, I found an old bag of mini-marshmallows. I quickly grabbed a few large handfuls and stuffed them in a snack-sized plastic bag, squeezed the air out, and sealed it. Voilá! DYI de-stresser ball! I tucked my homemade squishy ball into my jacket pocket and headed out the door.

Unfortunately, I had not anticipated the X-ray tech's request that I empty my pockets before my scan. I tried to quickly stuff my makeshift squishy ball behind my purse, but I'm pretty sure she saw it and is still wondering about the peculiar woman who carries around a snack-sized bag of mini-marshmallows.

How did I come to be this woman—a woman who frantically stuffs a bag of mini-marshmallows into her pocket before a doctor's appointment? I think the problem started with "being fine." Like many people recovering from crisis, when asked how I was doing, I'd say, "I'm fine." When friends asked me how they could help, I'd say, "I'm fine." But, like many people recovering from crisis, I was not, in fact, "fine."

The wisdom of Ecclesiastes is that we are not at all fine when we are trying to walk alone. Two are better than one, and three are better than two. Another person can offer us a hand to squeeze when staples are being removed; two friends can accompany us to the divorce lawyer's office; the whole church can work together to mow our lawn, clean our house, and pay our bills when our loved one is dying of cancer. As members of the body of Christ, we are called to bear the burdens of the weak and to be stronger together (Galatians 6:2).

Dear friend, let my mini-marshmallow tale be a lesson to you: don't be fine when you're not. Discover the peace and hope that come from asking for and receiving help. Let your burdens be borne by those called to carry them. One day, when you are "more fine," you will know the joy of extending a helping hand to someone who needs to squeeze it.

PRAYER

Dear Jesus,

We confess, we are often not "fine" as we walk through this season. Thank you for sending physical hands to hold us and help us in our time of need. Give us the courage to ask for and receive help. In your kind name we pray. AMEN.

FURTHER ENCOURAGEMENT

- Read Ecclesiastes 4:7–12; Galatians 6:2.

- Listen to "Kindness" by Sandra McCracken.

FOR REFLECTION

Do you have the tendency to say "I'm fine" when you're not? What specific help could you ask for or accept in this season?

NOTES

34

Another Helper

*And I will ask the Father, and he will give
you another Helper, to be with you forever.*
JOHN 14:16, ESV

ORPHANED AT AGE seven then adopted by a cruel distant cousin, Jane had often known deep distress in her life but rarely experienced the rescue of a helper. When her husband abandoned her with three young children, she naturally assumed that she would walk alone through this crisis. Like many of us, Jane, who was a Christian, failed to recognize the powerful Helper she had dwelling within her — the Holy Spirit.

Although we can't see this "other Helper," the Holy Spirit works mightily in us at all times and offers profound comfort in our times of need. Consider what Scripture tells us about the Holy Spirit:

The Holy Spirit, whom Jesus called the "Helper," was sent by God the Father and Jesus the Son to be our advocate, comforter, counselor, and friend. The Holy Spirit, our Helper, plays many roles in our lives as Christians.

Our Helper gives us new life in Christ (John 3:5–6; Ephesians 2:1): Our sin had killed our souls (Ephesians 2:1). The Holy

Spirit enlivened us in our spiritual death, giving birth to our new life in Christ.

Our Helper assures us that we are no longer orphans (Galatians 4:6): We are prone to forget the riches and resources we have as the children of God. In our heart, the Holy Spirit cries out, "Abba, Father," reminding us that we are never alone in our struggles.

Our Helper acts as the real presence of Christ in us at all times (John 14:16–17): The Holy Spirit is the *actual* presence of Christ in us, not just the *sense* of his presence. With Christ in us through the Spirit, nothing in this world can defeat us—not divorce, not disease, not even death, for Christ has overcome all the world's tribulations (Romans 8:35–39).

Our Helper comforts and counsels us (John 16:13): The Holy Spirit "[guides us] into all the truth" (John 16:13), helping us understand the Scriptures, reminding us of how God has rescued and redeemed in Jesus Christ, and giving us wisdom beyond human understanding. Such wonderful counsel deeply comforts us in the chaos and confusion of crisis.

Our Helper intercedes for us (Romans 8:26): The Holy Spirit knows precisely how to pray for us, supplying the words we need and praying according to the will of God (Romans 8:26–27).

Our Helper transforms us (2 Corinthians 3:17–18): The Holy Spirit dwells in us, pointing us constantly to the glory of Jesus, and in doing so, transforms us into his "glorious image" (2 Corinthians 3:18 NLT).

Dear friends, in this season of crisis, take comfort—you are not alone. Jesus has given you a most wonderful Helper,

Counselor, Guide, Advocate, and Comforter, to help you in the healing process.

PRAYER

Lord Jesus,

Thank you that you did not leave us alone but sent the perfect Helper. May we fully access the depths of the comfort the Spirit brings, the assurance that we are your children, the hope of your presence in us, the wise counsel and intercession, and best of all the transforming work that makes us more and more like you. AMEN.

FURTHER ENCOURAGEMENT

- Read John 14:15–17; 25–27; John 16:5–15; Romans 8:26–27; 2 Corinthians 3:17–18.

- Listen to "Holy Spirit, Living Breath of God" by Keith and Kristyn Getty.

FOR REFLECTION

In what ways have you known the help of the Holy Spirit during this season? What additional help might you ask of him?

NOTES

35

The God Who Is for You

What then shall we say to these things? If
God is for us, who can be against us?
ROMANS 8:31, ESV

WHEN MY FRIEND Peggy's husband was traveling and mine was on call, we often sat together at church. At almost six feet tall, she towered above me when we rose to sing. Her voice, strong and tender as her heart, soared above mine as she sang her favorite hymn, "It Is Well with My Soul." When Peggy was raped and murdered outside her home, the question that leapt from my lips was "Why?" Our pastor addressed this heart-felt question at her funeral: "While our hearts long to know 'why,' it seems that God is most interested in our knowing 'Who — Who is our God?'" Who, indeed, is this God? He is the God who is for us.

He is the King who created and rules over heaven and earth. Nothing happens to his beloved creation apart from his will (Isaiah 37:16).

He is the Mighty Warrior God who fights for his people, who carved a path right through the Red Sea to rescue the

Israelites then pitched the Egyptian horses and riders into that same sea (Exodus 15).

He is the Comforting God who speaks tenderly to Israel in the wilderness and sings comfort over his people when they return from their captivity in Babylon (Isaiah 40:1–3).

He is the Holy God, whose wrath we justly deserve but do not receive because he has showered his mercy and grace on us in Jesus Christ (Isaiah 6:1–7; Ephesians 2:3–5).

He is the Pursuing God, who, because of his steadfast love, went into the wilderness to allure his adulterous bride, the people of Israel, back to him (Hosea 2:14).

He is the Suffering God, who sent his own sinless Son to die for the forgiveness of our sins, who chose to be separated from his beloved Son in order to reconcile us to himself (John 3:16).

He is our Father God, our "Abba-Daddy" God, who quiets us with his love, who delights in us as his children (Galatians 4:6).

He is the Potter God, who places his hands in our muddiness and shapes us even through crisis and loss into the image of his Son (Isaiah 64:8).

And he is the Ever-present God, who is with us now in Christ and by his Spirit, and who awaits the day he will dwell with us forever (Revelation 21:3).

My friend Peggy's murder, which happened around thirty years ago, marked me deeply. But not for evil, as you might imagine. It marked me for good. I became more intimately acquainted with the God who is for us. I met mature believers — Peggy's parents — who knew this God so well and trusted him so deeply that they forgave her murderers. I learned from a faithful pastor to ask the question "who" even as the question "why" arises. I discovered the truth author Abby Hutto describes, "Suffering well takes faith in a God ... we cannot see and willingness to trust a plan we do not understand."[17]

PRAYER

Father God,

If you are "for us," nothing can stand against us.
Help us to cling to this truth more tightly than ever
in this season. In Jesus' name. AMEN.

FURTHER ENCOURAGEMENT

- Read Romans 8:31–39; Ephesians 2:3–5; Exodus 15.

- Listen to "It Is Well with My Soul" by Audrey Assad.

FOR REFLECTION

What aspects of God's character bring you comfort when you ask "why" about your suffering?

36

Go into Peace

*Daughter, your faith has made
you well; go in peace.*
LUKE 8:48, ESV

MAYBE IT'S BEEN twelve long years, and healing hasn't yet come.
Or maybe your child has been pronounced "cancer-free," but
your heart has yet to feel anxiety-free. When you live daily in
the distressing aftermath of disaster as the bleeding woman
in Luke 8 did, it may seem too risky to believe that Jesus will
make you well and bring you into his peace.

The day of the diagnosis has long since passed. The bleeding woman has now suffered with her illness for twelve trying
years. She has spent all her money on doctors, but none could
heal her. She has lost all community because she is considered
unclean (Luke 8:43). She's out of options. She is, frankly, desperate. Maybe that's why she reaches out to touch the healing
Rabbi's garment. Maybe desperation is what drives us all to
commit our wildest acts of faith.

Jesus, jostled and pressed by the throngs of people who have
come to see him, asks an odd, even preposterous question,
"Who touched me?" but no one fesses up (Luke 8:45). Peter,

ever ready to speak his mind, points out the absurdity of the question, but Jesus insists, "Someone has touched me, for I perceive that power has gone out from me" (Luke 8:45–46).

The once-bleeding woman, now healed, realizes she must confess. Trembling, she falls before Jesus, and right there in front of all those people, tells him her story, describes her years of illness, her years of loneliness. "I was desperate," she might have said. "And I was healed instantly" (Luke 8:47). As she finishes her confession and looks up, does she fear finding condemnation in the mighty Rabbi's eyes? After all, she, a woman, an unclean woman, had touched him, a man and a Rabbi.

But Jesus has no words of condemnation for her, only words of healing and forgiveness, words of peace, words of hope. "Daughter," he begins. He names her tenderly as his own. "Your faith has made you well." "Go in peace" he commands her. My pastor, Reverend Joel Treick, pointed out that the word translated "in" means literally "into" — "Go into peace." Jesus is inviting her "into peace, into a new life as a child of God, which would replace her old life of worry and despair over her chronic medical condition."[18] Because Jesus has healed all of our sins, we can now live into—and out of—his peace. Therein lies our deepest hope.

Dear friends, hear Jesus' call to trust him, to seek him in your sickness and exhaustion and stress. He has saved all who believe in him, and he has given us his peace. We may or may not know instantaneous healing or full recovery in the next few days or the next few years, but we will one day know them finally and forever. Until that day comes, let us in desperation reach for the hem of his garment and lean into the peace he gives.

PRAYER

Dear Jesus,

We are desperate to be healed; we aren't even strong enough to reach for you. Give us the faith we need. Help us to live into your peace, even when ongoing struggles threaten to unsettle us. In your healing name. AMEN.

FURTHER ENCOURAGEMENT

- Read Luke 8:42–48.

- Listen to "Heal Us Emmanuel" by Indelible Grace.

FOR REFLECTION

Imagine Jesus speaking directly to you, "Daughter (Son), your faith has made you well. Go into peace." Write out or pray aloud your response to those words.

NOTES

37

All We Like Sheep

He restores my soul. He leads me in paths
of righteousness for his name's sake.
PSALM 23:3, ESV

WHETHER YOUR CRISIS was brought on by your own sin, by another's sin, or by fallen world realities, you may find yourself acting like a sheep at times: confused, ignorant, wandering, helpless, lost. According to the *Dictionary of Biblical Imagery*, "Sheep are not only dependent creatures; they are also singularly unintelligent, prone to wandering, and unable to find their way to a sheep fold even when it is within sight."[19]

The prophet Isaiah tells us that we are all like sheep, going astray, turning to our own way (Isaiah 53:6). In our discomfort after a crisis, we often seek easy relief, tripping down paths of our own devises, making plans to make things right. Before long, we stumble into the path of predators eager to attack us in our vulnerable state. We may give in to the temptation to numb ourselves through food, drink, or other substances. We may be unable to resist the temptation to move forward when God has said to wait. Before long, we land upside down, like a miserable fallen sheep trapped on its back by its own wooly weight.

Like the miserable sheep, belly-up in our own sin, we are helpless to right ourselves. The apostle Paul puts it bluntly, "And you were dead in your trespasses and sins in which you once walked" (Ephesians 2:1–2). In our sinful state, we needed something beyond recovery; we required regeneration, a new life altogether. Because of our desperate sheepishness, God sent a Lamb, his own Lamb, his own spotless sacrifice. On this Lamb, our sin was laid.

"He was oppressed, and he was afflicted, yet he opened not his mouth; like a lamb that is led to the slaughter, and like a sheep that before its shearers is silent, so he opened not his mouth" (Isaiah 53:7). The bad news—God's Lamb was slaughtered— leads to good news—our restoration hope. Out of the anguish of his soul (Isaiah 53:11), Jesus restored our soul (Psalm 23:3). Jesus accomplished for us what we could not accomplish on our own: he returned us to God. He raised us to new life in him. He restored, refreshed, and revived us.

Now we seek the voice and protection of our Shepherd. Our Shepherd leads us beside "waters of rest," where we drink fully of his goodness. Our Shepherd supplies all of our needs; lacking nothing, we rest like a baby satisfied by its mother's milk. Our Shepherd leads us on "right paths," turning us away from the sin-ruts we would dig for ourselves. As we settle into our Shepherd's path, we wear his righteousness, and he receives the glory due his name. This is the restoration our souls long for.

Our Dear Shepherd,

We confess our waywardness to you; we acknowledge that we have entrenched ourselves in self-dug paths. We thank you for your perfect sacrifice for us, for restoring our soul. Help us to trust you and follow you in your right paths for the sake of your glory. AMEN.

FURTHER ENCOURAGEMENT

- Read Isaiah 53:6–12.

- Listen to "The King of Love My Shepherd Is" by Mass of the Rock.

FOR REFLECTION

In what ways do you feel like a sheep right now? How does Jesus' restoration of your soul give you hope?

NOTES

38

Your Kingdom Come

Your kingdom come, your will be
done, on earth as it is in heaven.
MATTHEW 6:10, ESV

AS WE SURVEY the ruins of a marriage after an affair, a neighborhood after a flood, a world after a global pandemic, the cry that rises naturally to our lips is, "Your kingdom come." What do we mean when we pray this prayer—whose kingdom is it, what is that kingdom like, and what will it mean for this kingdom to come?

Whose kingdom is it? It is God's kingdom, the kingdom of the One who created heaven and earth and declared it "very good" (Genesis 1:31). Although God's original creation was deeply damaged by sin, because of his "holy stubbornness," his "refusal to accept ruin,"[20] God repaired the broken creation in the most unlikely of ways, by becoming man and dying on a cross.

God's kingdom is characterized by shalom: "heavenly wholeness, the right alignment of everything" and the belief that shalom is "not beyond recovery."[21] It is the realm of grace that announces the rule of grace. In this kingdom, the righting and restoring of all things began with Christ's death and res-urrection. When our King returns, this kingdom will be fully consummated, with shalom reigning forever in the now-re-stored new heavens and new earth.

God's kingdom is the kingdom of heaven that opposes itself to the kingdom of darkness. To pray "Your kingdom come" is to pray that Jesus would today defeat the wily efforts of Satan, the prince of darkness who seeks to captivate our attention and energy for his purposes (Colossians 1:13; Ephesians 2:2). Christ the King has already triumphed over the god of this world on the cross; one day, he will return to establish his kingdom and cast Satan into the lake of fire forever (Revelation 20:10).

To pray "your kingdom come" is to repent of our own ten-dencies to create small kingdoms by placing ourselves, our loved ones, our work, our homes, or any other thing we see as ours, on the throne of our lives. It is to pray, "Your kingdom come and rule in my heart; your will, not mine, be done in my life."

To pray "your kingdom come" is to seek to serve our King by fulfilling our mission to grow and multiply his beauty on this earth today. It is to move toward an ex-wife in the hope of co-parenting in harmony; it is to pull out moldy drywall in the hope of restoring a flooded home; it is to care for the sick and broken in the hope of healing soul, if not body.

As we recover from crisis, it is easy to recognize the disas-ter this world has become through the ravages of sin. To pray "your kingdom come" is a daring prayer, an imaginative prayer, a prayer that acknowledges the gap between what is and what ought to be. And yet, every day, we must persist in praying it, in announcing to the world, "Our King has come; he will one day come again." And when he does, shalom will reign forever.

PRAYER

Our Father,

Your kingdom come. May your reign of grace be the rule of the day. In the name of Christ our King. AMEN.

FURTHER ENCOURAGEMENT

- Read Matthew 6:7–15.
- Listen to "King of Love" by Steven Curtis Chapman.

FOR REFLECTION

Into what broken places would you like to see God's kingdom come?

39

Instead of Ashes

To all who mourn in Israel, he will
give a crown of beauty for ashes.
ISAIAH 61:3, NLT

VICTIMS WHO LOST their homes to wildfires in California report varying experiences of mourning. One woman tears up whenever she sees someone wearing a Laker's sweatshirt like the one she lost in the fire. Another aches at the loss of the home where she and her now-deceased husband raised their three children. A third says she misses the goats she farmed on her acreage. Whatever disaster we experience, it is normal to mourn our losses. Into our grief and mourning, Isaiah speaks hope for restoration, revival, and renewal.

Isaiah warns Israel about the pending consequences of their rebellion—exile to Babylon. Yet, even as Isaiah prophesies the coming disaster, he shares the good news of a coming day of restoration. In Isaiah 61, Isaiah announces that one day the Anointed One will come. This Anointed One, Jesus, speaks directly to his people, describing his mission. Imagine the Lord Jesus speaking these words to you, saying something like this,

I've come to bring you good news, riches for your poverty, healing for your broken heart (Isaiah 61:1).

I've come to free you from the prison of abuse and oppression as well as the prison of your own sin (Isaiah 61:1).

I've come to destroy your worst enemy, the evil one, and all who have done harm in his name (Isaiah 61:2).

I've come to comfort everyone who mourns. That includes those who mourn their own sin and those who mourn the sins of others. That includes those who mourn loved ones lost early to death, family homes lost to disaster (Isaiah 61:2–3).

I've come to bring you out of exile, to take you to your forever home with your loving Father (Isaiah 61:4).

Imagine the comfort of such words whispered into your broken heart by the Lord Jesus himself. He has more good news:

Instead of ashes of mourning smeared on your head, you will wear a bejeweled crown befitting the bride of Christ (Isaiah 61:3).

Instead of streaks of tears sullying your face, your face will shine with the oil of gladness and the hope of restoration (Isaiah 61:3).

Instead of tattered rags of despair, you will wear robes of your Redeemer's righteousness (Isaiah 61:3).

No longer shriveled by sin and sadness, you will stand strong, planted firmly in the Lord's steadfast love, like a mighty oak waving its leaf-laden branches in praise of the Lord's glory (Isaiah 61:3).

The ruins of your life will be rebuilt, losses to the evil one will be restored, relationships ravaged by sin will be revived (Isaiah 61:4).

Dear friends, if you are mourning now, take heart. Jesus, the Anointed One, has already come to comfort you. A day is surely coming when your temporary mourning will give way to eternal gladness, for in our forever home, there will be no more mourning or sadness or death (Revelation 21:4).

PRAYER

Lord,

As we wait for the day when you will anoint us with the oil of gladness and crown us with your beauty, help us to seek and know your comfort. In the name of our Anointed Savior. AMEN.

FURTHER ENCOURAGEMENT

- Read Isaiah 61:1–4

- Listen to "There Will Be a Great Rejoicing" by Thad Cockrell.

FOR REFLECTION

List some things that you miss or feel sad about in this season. Ask God to bring comfort to you in this mourning.

NOTES

40

But God Intended It for Good

*You intended to harm me, but God intended
it all for good. He brought me to this position
so I could save the lives of many people.*
GENESIS 50:20, NLT

WHO INTENDED TO harm you? Was it a co-worker, whose lies led to your job loss? Or an abuser, whose touch stole your innocence? Or maybe there was no clear agent of harm in your crisis—maybe you have no one to blame for the baby taken from your womb before its time or the tornado that tore through your home?

Joseph, the man who spoke the words, "You intended to harm me, but God intended it all for good," was well-acquainted with harm. As a teenager, his father's favoritism and his own narcissism set him up for disaster (Genesis 37). His brothers, about whom he had given a bad report to his father and with whom he had shared his dream of ruling over them, so despised him that they first threw him in a well and later pulled him out to sell him into slavery (Genesis 37:2, 5–8, 12–28).

In the coming years, Joseph would face even more trials. And yet, the song line of God's redemption in the midst of crisis would hum steadily through his life:

- Brought to Egypt as a slave, Joseph would know success because of the Lord's redeeming work in and through him: "The Lord was with Joseph…. the Lord caused all he did to succeed in his hands" (Genesis 39:2–3).

- Falsely accused of rape by his Egyptian master's wife and thrown into prison, Joseph would again be met with the Lord's love and grace: "But the Lord was with Joseph and showed him steadfast love and gave him favor in the sight of the keeper of the prison" (Genesis 39:21).

- After years in prison, finally released to interpret Pharaoh's dream, Joseph would rise to second-in-command over all of Egypt, again because of the Lord's work in him: "Then Pharaoh said to Joseph, 'Since God has shown you all this, there is none so discerning and wise as you are. You shall be over my house…'" (Genesis 41:39–40).

Through each crisis, Joseph was met by the Lord's grace, favor, power, and presence. As he discovered the Lord's goodness to him in the midst of crisis, Joseph was transformed: he became a humble, grateful man. When his two sons were born, he asserted, "For God has made me fruitful in the land of my affliction" (Genesis 41:52). It is this humility and gratitude that allowed him to forgive his brothers when they were reunited.

Just as the Lord transformed Joseph through crisis, he transforms us. Let us, with Joseph, keep our eyes open to the bigger story, the story of redemption, that God is writing even in our worst stories of harm.

PRAYER

Redeeming God,

Help us to trace your redemption through the harm we have suffered. Help us to look beyond present difficult circumstances to imagine the good you are working even today. In Jesus' redeeming name. AMEN.

FURTHER ENCOURAGEMENT

- Read Joseph's story, found in Genesis 37; 39–50.

- Listen to "Where No One Stands Alone" by Alison Krauss and The Cox Family.

FOR REFLECTION

Can you see any good that God has already done or that he might intend to do through your suffering?

NOTES

41

Quick Fixes and Faith Healings

*Heal me, O Lord, and I shall be healed; save
me, and I shall be saved, for you are my praise.*
JEREMIAH 17:14, ESV

A FRIEND DIAGNOSED with cancer was offered actual snake
oil to shrink her tumor. Quadriplegic Joni Eareckson Tada
recounts multiple conversations with people who asked her
if she had sought healing prayer. Both my friend and Joni fell
victim to people who long to believe in quick fixes for complex
problems. Recovery is rarely quick and only occasionally easy.

It is not that quick fixes and faith healings, or, what might
better be called miracles, don't happen in Scripture; they certainly do:

- When the Egyptians are pursuing the Israelites, the
  Lord parts the Red Sea so the Israelites can cross safely
  (Exodus 14:15–31). Daniel is saved from being eaten by
  lions (Daniel 6:16–22); Jonah is rescued after being swal-
  lowed by a sea-monster (Jonah 1:17–2:10). These are just
  a few of numerous Old Testament miracles.

- In the New Testament, Jesus performs as many as forty miracles. Jesus calms the sea (Matthew 8:23–27), feeds five thousand (Matthew 14:15–22), raises a widow's son (Luke 7:11–15), and heals a hemorrhaging woman (Matthew 9:20–22).

While Scripture records many miracles and healings, it shares equally as many stories of people waiting for healing and restoration:

- In the Old Testament, we find people waiting long years for God's promises to be fulfilled or for restoration to come. Sarah and Abraham wait ten years for their promised child to be born; she is ninety and he is ninety-nine when Isaac finally arrives (Genesis 17:17). Joseph spends two years in an Egyptian jail, waiting to be remembered by the cupbearer whose dream he interpreted (Genesis 41).

- The New Testament also gives examples of people whose problems are not quickly resolved, people of faith who are not healed. The apostle Paul prays three times for his "thorn in the flesh" (an unspecified ailment) to be removed, but it is not; instead, he is given grace to endure. (2 Corinthians 12:7–9).

- In the Garden of Gethsemane, Jesus prays that the cup of suffering might pass from him (Luke 22:39–44). But hours later, he is dying on a cross. Jesus could not be spared; he had to die for our sins.

What then do we learn about quick fixes and faith healings? Joni Eareckson Tada offers her answer: though God has not relieved her from her quadriplegia, he has healed and restored in other ways: "My affliction has stretched my hope, made me know Christ better...led me to repentance of sin, increased my faith, and strengthened my character."[22]

Dear friends, be assured: while the Lord's healing and restoration may not come in the time or manner we expect it, we can be sure, because of Christ, that it will come.

PRAYER

Jesus, our Healer and Restorer,

We confess, we tend to want things done our way in our time. Remind us that you bore the cross for us so we may one day be fully healed and finally restored. AMEN.

FURTHER ENCOURAGEMENT

- Read Romans 5:3–5; Mark 1:29–39.

- Listen to "Blessings" by Laura Story.

FOR REFLECTION

What healing and restoration have you longed for during your crisis? How have you seen that come to pass? How have you seen healing and restoration other than what you expected?

NOTES

42

Scar Tissue

Do not regard lightly the discipline of the
Lord, nor be weary when reproved by him.
HEBREWS 12:7, ESV

SCAR TISSUE CAN wreak havoc in recovery from any surgery, but particularly shoulder surgery. Unfortunately, I am prone to scarring. After each of my five shoulder surgeries, I had to submit to what is sometimes humorously nicknamed "physical torture," the efforts of skilled physical therapists to break up the stubborn nemesis of scar tissue.

It is not only surgery that threatens to scar us. The wounds of racism, divorce, abuse, betrayal, and bullying can leave scars that bind our hearts relationally. Natural disasters and bad diagnoses can have similar effects. All crises threaten to harden our hearts with scar tissue if we turn to little-g gods in our pain. Whenever we trust in the seeming safety of cynicism, the self-protection of isolation, or the numbing of substances, we are in danger. When our hearts become hardened, we are not free to live and love in the freedom Christ has won for us.

If scar tissue begins to form, we need outside help to free us from the entanglements of our hearts: "Endure hardship as discipline; God is treating you as his children.... If you are not disciplined—and everyone undergoes discipline—then you are not legitimate, not true sons and daughters at all" (Hebrews 12:7–8 NIV). The Lord's discipline, while it may be painful, is sometimes necessary to our recovery.

Just as my physical therapist had to stretch my shoulder and apply pressure that felt painful at the time, the Lord's discipline may feel painful as we experience it: "For the moment all discipline seems painful rather than pleasant..." (Hebrews 12:11). Just as my physical therapist had my healing and recovery in mind when he caused me pain, the Lord has our healing from sin and restoration to wholeness in Christ in mind when he corrects us: "but later it yields the peaceful fruit of righteousness to those who have been trained by it" (Hebrews 12:11).

As the author of Hebrews reminds us, the Lord disciplines us as a heavenly Father who loves his children. After all, he points out, we have not been punished for our sins by the Father's wrath. It was the Father's own sinless Son who "endured the cross, despising the shame," taking God's wrath on himself (Hebrews 12:2). Now we, as God's children, can endure the loving discipline and sometimes painful correction of the Father, knowing that it will soften our hearts, freeing us from the scar tissue that often binds us. As he does his restorative work in us, we will become more and more like Jesus, freed to enjoy and serve God and to enjoy and serve others as he designed us to do.

PRAYER

Heavenly Father,

Even though we don't always understand your discipline, help us to receive it as a good gift from a good Father. Help us to see our current trials as your tool for breaking up our hardness of heart. Free us to enjoy and serve you. In Jesus' enduring name. AMEN.

FURTHER ENCOURAGEMENT

- Read Hebrews 12:1–11.

- Listen to "Though You Slay Me" by Shane and Shane.

FOR REFLECTION

What painful circumstances are you enduring? How might the Lord be using these painful circumstances to heal and restore you?

NOTES

43

A Purpose for Your Pain

He comforts us in all our troubles so that
we can comfort others. When they are
troubled, we will be able to give them
the same comfort God has given us.
2 CORINTHIANS 1:4, NLT

ON THE FIRST night of her divorce support group's fall session, Luisa arrived early and stood near the door, her bright eyes ready to welcome all who entered. By her own admission, she was nothing like the shamed and shriveled woman who had first entered that room several years before. As Luisa told me, "When my husband left me for a younger woman, I thought the loneliness and fear would actually kill me."

But a persistent friend who had also lost her husband to adultery and divorce continued to invite Luisa to her church's divorce support group. Finally, Luisa had visited. There, she had met the comfort of Christ in people who knew how to offer it because they had suffered similarly. Over time, in this comforting community, she began to heal and regain hope. Now, she loved nothing more than reaching out to others who limped into the group, feeling like they might die from the pain.

Luisa now owned and lived the truth that Paul proclaims in his beautiful letter to the Corinthians: "He comforts us in all our troubles *so that*…. we will be able to give them the same comfort God has given us" (2 Corinthians 1:4–5 NLT). Paul does not offer the trite words, "I know how you feel" to those in affliction. Instead, he reminds us that he and his ministry partners have themselves suffered, so severely that they "expected to die" (2 Corinthians 1:9 NLT). And yet, as they "despaired of life itself," they discovered another of God's purposes for their pain: they learned to rely not on themselves but on the God "who raises the dead" (2 Corinthians 1:9 NLT). Having seen how God rescued him from disaster and death, Paul could in turn, assure all future sufferers of the comfort in Christ God provides.

Paul continues, reminding us that our pain holds not only a purpose but also a promise: "For the more we suffer for Christ, the more God will shower us with his comfort through Christ" (2 Corinthians 1:5 NLT). It's a gospel cycle: we suffer; God comforts; we comfort others; they learn to "patiently endure" (2 Corinthians 1:6 NLT). As they patiently endure, they in turn comfort others with the comfort they have received in Christ. In God's economy, comfort is multiplied.

Dear friends, take heart. In your pain, the Lord will bring the comfort of Christ to you; one day you will know the deep and abiding joy of bringing that comfort to others. Your pain will never be without purpose.

PRAYER

Father of All Mercies and God of All Comfort,

Thank you for comforting us in our season of suffering. Thank you for the profound privilege of sharing that comfort with others. Help us take that risk today, to offer the comfort of Christ to one who desperately needs it. In Christ's name. AMEN.

FURTHER ENCOURAGEMENT

- Read 2 Corinthians 1:3–11.

- Listen to "May the Mind of Christ My Savior" by Dust Company.

FOR REFLECTION

In what ways have you seen God allow you to minister to others because of the pain you have experienced? How has doing so encouraged you?

NOTES

44

Good News of Great Joy

*Fear not, for behold, I bring you good news
of great joy that will be for all the people.*
LUKE 2:10, ESV

PEOPLE HUNCH OVER their phones and devices, scrolling, scrolling, scrolling, desperately seeking some good news, but they find only dire reports. They learn that the death toll has doubled, that hundreds of thousands may die in the United States alone, that the economy will fail if the shutdown continues. All seems bleak today, in the second week of the global pandemic. When crisis brings bad news day after day, we can look to another bleak season of history, when God had not spoken with his people for four hundred years. Into that bleak and silent season, angels arrived, making multiple announcements of "good news of great joy for all the people" (Luke 2:10).

God first sends the angel Gabriel to Zechariah, an old priest, with good news that lays the groundwork for the best news. Gabriel frightens Zechariah as he fulfills his priestly duty in the sanctuary and tells him his long-prayed prayer has been answered: his barren wife, Elizabeth, will have a baby. "And you will have joy and gladness, and many will rejoice at his birth" (Luke 1:13–14). This long-looked-for child will prepare the hearts of the people for their Savior to come. Sadly, Zechariah struggles to believe such impossibly good news, and he is struck silent until the baby John arrives.

God next sends the angel Gabriel to Mary, a young engaged Israelite virgin, with the astounding news that she will give birth to the Savior (Luke 1:29–33). Like Zechariah, Mary is at first frightened by the angel and "confused and disturbed" by his message of favor. Gabriel urges her not to fear and points her to the miracle-pregnancy of her cousin Elizabeth, saying, "For nothing will be impossible with God" (Luke 1:36–37). Though still confused and likely concerned about what her betrothed will think, Mary receives God's message of good news with faith and hope. After visiting her now-pregnant cousin, Mary sings a song of praise, rejoicing in the many great things her Savior has done and will do for his people (Luke 1:46–55).

Finally, God sends first one angel and then a whole host of angels to seemingly unlikely recipients — shepherds, the most ordinary of ordinary people in the most out of the way place. The angel urges them too not to fear and then tells them the reason for rejoicing, "I bring you good news of great joy that will be for all the people" (Luke 2:10). The shepherds, excited by the good news, hurry off to Bethlehem to see their Savior.

The silence has been broken for thousands of years now. Our Savior has come to the earth in flesh. Our Savior has died for our sins. Our Savior has risen to new life. What good news indeed, for "all people," for anyone who believes in him. Let us rejoice in this good news, running to see our newborn Savior, remembering our risen Savior, and keeping our eye out for our returning Savior. This good news brings the greatest joy even on the worst days.

Lord, God,

Thank you for breaking that silence so long ago with such extraordinary good news. Help us to hear and receive this good news with great joy. In Jesus' saving name. AMEN.

FURTHER ENCOURAGEMENT

- Read Luke 1–2:20.

- Listen to "My Soul Magnifies the Lord" by Chris Tomlin.

FOR REFLECTION

In what way is the news of Jesus' birth, life, death, resurrection, and ultimate return good news to you in the midst of crisis?

NOTES

45

Surrender

Behold, I am the servant of the Lord. Let
it be to me according to your word.
LUKE 1:38, ESV

MANY OF US in crisis know the sense of being called to die to hopes and dreams we long cherished. Mary, the mother of Jesus, encourages us in this hard place. There is perhaps no agony like the agony a mother feels when her child suffers. Whether the child suffers through their own failings and sin or through the harm inflicted by another, a mother flinches at every punishing blow. Mary is no exception.

Her story begins with a profound expression of faith and hope in the Lord. She is a young girl, possibly fourteen to sixteen years old, when the angel Gabriel appears to her, disrupting her simple life. After encouraging her not to be afraid because she has found favor with the Lord, Gabriel reveals that she will give birth to the Messiah (Luke 1:30–33).

Indeed, Mary has every reason to be afraid. It is no easy task to become the mother of the Messiah. The unplanned pregnancy, like many today, would have aroused fear. Would her betrothed, Joseph, abandon her? Would she be left helpless and alone? And yet, Mary surrenders, declaring herself a servant of the Lord and proclaiming, "Let it be to me according to your word" (Luke 1:38).

In the years to come, though, Mary will wrestle with her son's calling. She feels deep distress when Jesus, twelve at the time, disappears for three days, and is eventually found sitting with the teachers in the temple (Luke 2:48). Many years later, she attempts, along with Jesus' brothers, to call him away from ministering to the crowds. On that day, she hears Jesus' heart-shearing message, "Who is my mother, and who are my brothers?" (Matthew 12:48). Yes, Mary suffered.

Whatever you have felt in your season of crisis—confusion, doubt, distress—Mary felt it too. Despite her earliest words of surrender, she eventually realized that mothering the Messiah meant standing by helplessly as he went about saving the world according to his plan, not hers. If she were to continue to follow Jesus, Mary had to decide—would she yield control of her life (and his) to her Savior, God's Son, the Messiah? Would she follow Jesus to the foot of the cross? In crisis, we face the same decision.

Mary does decide to follow Jesus to the foot of the cross. We find her standing beneath him as his body, bloodied and beaten, hangs, dying. As unbearable as this moment must have been for Mary, she is there. In her presence there and in her presence with the disciples in the coming days and years, we see her surrender to Jesus, her settled acceptance of his way of salvation.

Crisis and recovery compel us to consider: will we trust Jesus even when his way feels like death? Mary's surrender draws us to hope that there is life beyond the cross. There is resurrection. There is restoration. May we dare to believe that in our moment of misery, there can be everlasting joy.

PRAYER

Lord Jesus,

Help us to surrender to your loving way even when it feels like death. Give us glimpses of your joy even in our sorrows. In your resurrected name. AMEN.

FURTHER ENCOURAGEMENT

- Read Luke 1:26–38; Luke 2:41–52; John 19:25–27.

- Listen to "Be Born in Me" by Francesca Battistelli.

FOR REFLECTION

What would it look like for you to surrender to Jesus in this season?

46

The Rest of Restoration

And on the seventh day God finished
all the work that he had done, and
he rested on the seventh day from
all his work that he had done.
GENESIS 2:2, ESV

THE FIRST TIME I recovered from shoulder surgery, I was blindsided by the fatigue. My limbs hung limp, heavy and sluggish; my nerves were frenzied by pain. Restful sleep eluded me. Meanwhile, the items on my to-do list stacked up in direct proportion to my incapacitation. Recovery fatigue set in; what I desperately needed was rest.

On the seventh day of creation, after God had placed the finishing touches on his masterpiece—his image-bearers, he rested (Genesis 2:2). God rested because his work, his plan, his purpose, was fully accomplished. The Lord rested as only the ruler of the cosmos can rest.

The Lord designed his image-bearers for rest and called them to receive this gift: "Six days you shall labor, and do all your work, but the seventh day is a Sabbath to the Lord your God. On it you shall not do any work…" (Deuteronomy 5:12–14).

The Lord knew that we needed rest; the Lord knew that to experience this rest, we would need to trust him completely.

What are you to do, though, when the housework piles up but you can't lift your arm after shoulder surgery? When soggy carpets need to be stripped before mold sets in after the flood? When sleep won't come because you're worried about the child support check? Surely you can't just do nothing?

God set a Sabbath rhythm: to work and to rest, to work and to rest. We may not be able to do the housework, but we can ask for help from others, and we can rest in receiving. We can strip the carpets, but then we must rest from that work. And as far as the child support check, there is a time to pursue and a time to pray, there is a time to trust, and a time to wait on God's provision.

In addition to physical, mental, and emotional rest, we desperately need the rest of restoration provided by Jesus. As Richard D. Phillips explains, "If you have put your faith in this saving God, if you have trusted his gospel in Jesus Christ, you now can rest.... You can face the prospect of loss in this life, of suffering, and even of death, for ours is the God of the Sabbath, who established his purposes forever from the beginning. Through faith in him you enter into his rest."[23]

Dear friend, in this season of weight and weariness, hear the call of the One who has bought with his life the rest you crave. Come to Jesus, who invites you to the rest of restoration.

Father, God,

Thank you for your Sabbath rest, and thank you for the ultimate rest granted in Jesus. Help us to come to you for every kind of rest we need in our recovery. AMEN.

FURTHER ENCOURAGEMENT

- Read Genesis 2:1–3; Exodus 20:8–11; Hebrews 4:9–10.

- Listen to "Good to Me" by Audrey Assad.

FOR REFLECTION

In what ways are you struggling with the need for rest or the inability to rest? Write a short letter to God about what things you need to entrust to him so you can gain needed rest.

NOTES

47

Grieving with Hope

Brothers and sisters, we do not want you
to be uninformed about those who sleep
in death, so that you do not grieve like the
rest of mankind, who have no hope.
1 THESSALONIANS 4:13, NIV

IN HER MEMOIR, *Choosing to See,* Mary Beth Chapman describes "With Hope," the song her husband Steven Curtis wrote for friends after their daughter died: "It's a testimony to a family we watched grieve with the hope of a living Comforter, a brave family who daily confirmed through their pain and tears that they would see their little girl again."[24] Ten years after Steven Curtis wrote that song, the Chapmans' precious five-year-old daughter Maria died in a tragic accident. The Chapmans would, like their friends, grieve with great hope, assured that their daughter was in heaven with Jesus, happier than she'd ever been.

The apostle Paul, writing to the Thessalonians to emphasize the good news of the second coming of Jesus, urges them not to grieve as those who have no hope. To grieve with hope, the Thessalonians, and we ourselves, need to understand death and resurrection and the final resurrection. Paul names two crucial truths that help us grieve with hope.

First, Paul tells us to be informed "about those who are asleep…" (1 Thessalonians 4:13). What does he mean? As John Stott explains, by using the word "sleep," Paul emphasizes that "death is only temporary. As sleep is followed by awakening, so death will be followed by resurrection."[25] The body may remain in the grave or in the crematorium, but the believer's soul will be conscious, present with Jesus. Jesus says to the repentant thief on the cross, "Today you will be with me in Paradise" (Luke 23:43). Knowing that our beloveds' believing souls are immediately reunited with Jesus after death gives us profound hope as we grieve.

Second, Paul tells us what will happen to the dead when Jesus returns: "For since we believe that Jesus died and rose again, even so, through Jesus, God will bring with him those who have fallen asleep" (1 Thessalonians 4:14). One day, when Jesus returns, he will raise the bodies of the dead. Then he will raise the living, and we will together go to meet Christ and escort him back to earth where he will establish his kingdom: the new heavens and the new earth (1 Thessalonians 4:17).

While many details about death and resurrection and that final day remain a mystery, this much we know: one day, all who trust in Christ will be with him forever, bodies and souls fully restored. Even as we grieve the loss of loved ones today, we have every reason to grieve with hope.

Risen Lord,

Thank you for reminding us of what is true about our loved ones lost to death. Help us to see them in heaven with you, rejoicing in you and enjoying fellowship with you. Help us to grieve with hope as we await the day when we will be rejoined with you and with them. In your resurrecting name. AMEN.

FURTHER ENCOURAGEMENT

- Read 1 Thessalonians 4:13–18; 1 Corinthians 15:35–49.

- Listen to "See" by Steven Curtis Chapman.

FOR REFLECTION

How does knowing what happens after death help you as you grieve?

NOTES

(48)

I Believe/Help My Unbelief

Lord, I believe; help my unbelief.
MARK 9:24, ESV

THE FATHER HAD lost hope that his son would ever recover. For years the young man had been violently abused by an "unclean spirit," thrown to the ground, jerked around, and left foaming at the mouth. The father had asked the disciples to heal his son, but they "were not able" (Mark 9:18). The father is at his breaking point when he begs Jesus for help, "If you can do anything, have compassion on us and help us" (Mark 9:22). Like many of us who have spent years waiting for recovery to come, the father's faith wavers: "I believe; help my unbelief" (Mark 9:24).

The good news of Scripture is that Jesus meets us right where we are, right in the space of our faltering faith. He heals the faith-faltering-father's son. In the well-known story of the so-called "doubting Thomas," Jesus also responds compassionately to a wavering faith. As we consider Thomas' story, we discover that we have every reason to hope when our faith wavers, because Jesus meets our faithlessness with his faithful love.

The other disciples had seen the risen Christ. They told Thomas, "We have seen the Lord" (John 20:25). But Thomas wasn't buying it. Maybe he was a "doubter." Or maybe he was just so bitterly disappointed he couldn't bear to hope anymore. He bluntly told the other disciples, "Unless I see in his hands the mark of the nails, and place my finger into the mark of the nails, and place my hand into his side, I will never believe" (John 20:25). Really, Thomas, *never*?!

The next eight days must have been long for Thomas, who seemed to have temporarily lost his faith. Think how he must have suffered in his bitter sorrow while the other disciples rejoiced that Jesus was alive. And then, imagine—Jesus is suddenly standing in a locked room right in the circle of Thomas and the others. "Peace be with you," Jesus says, by way of greeting (John 20:26).

Instead of chiding Thomas for his disbelief, Jesus invites him to touch the mark of the nails, to see his hands, to "put out your hand, and place it in my side," echoing Thomas' words back to him (John 20:25, 27). Jesus urges Thomas, "Do not disbelieve, but believe" (John 20:27). In that moment, Thomas sees Jesus for who he really and truly is, professing, "My Lord and my God!" (John 20:28).

Then Jesus speaks the words often heard as a reprimand of Thomas: "Have you believed because you have seen me? Blessed are those who have not seen and yet have believed" (John 20:29). But certainly, Jesus describes the blessing of all of his future followers, those who will believe though we will never see his nail-scarred hands or put our hands in his wounds.

Dear friends, what hope we have when our faith falters! The very presence of Jesus resides in us by his Spirit to remind us of what is true. Today, if crisis is causing your faith to waver, hear Jesus calling to you, "Do not disbelieve but believe."

PRAYER

Lord, Jesus,

We believe; help our unbelief. Thank you for loving us faithfully and strengthening our faith when we falter. In your faithful name. AMEN.

FURTHER ENCOURAGEMENT

- Read Mark 9:14–29; John 20:24–29.

- Listen to "Help My Unbelief" by Indelible Grace.

FOR REFLECTION

Has your faith wavered at times during this season? How do these two stories encourage you?

NOTES

$$\left(49 \right)$$

The Lord's Perfect Timing

The Lord is not slow to fulfill his promise as
some count slowness, but is patient toward
you, not wishing that any should perish,
but that all should reach repentance.
2 PETER 3:9, ESV

WHEN OUR SON had three surgeries in a four-week period for a brain tumor, we often wondered about the Lord's timing and his ways. Our son's first brain surgery was halted two hours in — more diagnostic testing was needed to determine if the tumor was in fact a tumor. Further testing confirmed the original diagnosis, and two weeks later, he had a second surgery — ninety-eight percent of the tumor was removed. Ten days later, the wound became infected, and our son had a third surgery, to remove infected bone in the skull cap. He was then placed on an eight-week course of antibiotics and scheduled for a fourth surgery six months later to implant a synthetic skull cap. We were, frankly, bewildered, at the Lord's timing and his way of answering our prayers.

Addressing first century Christians who, in their suffering, felt impatient for the Lord's second coming, Peter assures them that the Lord's timing is accurate to the millisecond: "The Lord is not slow to fulfill his promise…" (2 Peter 3:9). In waiting to return, the Lord is growing patience in believers and showing patience to unbelievers.

How does God grow patience in believers as we wait on his timing? Patience, according to Karen Swallow Prior, is the "willingness to endure suffering."[26] To wait is, at some level, to suffer. As we wait for our suffering to end, our patience — our capacity to endure suffering — grows. And as that capacity grows, our desire to live a holy life in anticipation of the joys of restoration life intensifies (2 Peter 3:11–13).

By waiting to return, the Lord is also showing his patience toward the as-yet unrepentant: "[He] is patient toward you, not wishing that any should perish, but that all should reach repentance" (2 Peter 3:9). When Christ comes, any who do not trust in Christ as Savior will be sentenced to eternal punishment (2 Thessalonians 1:5–9). Our perfectly patient Lord waits to dwell with his people so that more will turn to him and trust in him.

While our son was enduring his first three brain surgeries, my father, our son's namesake, was dying of late stage cancer. I had never been certain if he truly trusted in Christ. After our son's third surgery, when we learned his tumor was not cancerous, my father texted me five words, "To God be the glory." Eleven days later, he died. I believe that our son's protracted and agonizing journey made my father desperate. I believe, weakened by cancer and powerless to help his grandson, he turned to the Lord as his only hope.

When God's timing does not suit ours, we can trust him. He is showing patience to the perishing and patience with the professing. One thing we know: his timing is always perfect.

PRAYER

Father,

Thank you for your perfect patience with us and with others. Help us to wait on you with joy and hope. In Jesus' compassionate name. AMEN.

FURTHER ENCOURAGEMENT

- Read 2 Peter 3:1–13; 2 Thessalonians 1:5–9.

- Listen to "Oh God Our Help in Ages Past" by Sojourn.

FOR REFLECTION

How do you think the Lord might be growing or showing patience through his timing?

NOTES

50

Our Tear-Wiping Father

He will wipe away every tear from their eyes,
and death shall be no more, neither shall there
be mourning, nor crying, nor pain anymore,
for the former things have passed away.
REVELATION 21:4, ESV

MAYBE YOUR MOTHER chided you for wasting tears over the father who abandoned your family when you were five. Maybe a well-meaning pastor urged you to dry your eyes because your husband of forty years was now with Jesus. Or maybe kids at school mocked you for crying when they bullied you day after day, and you vowed you would never cry again.

Crisis has a way of making us feel ambivalent about our tears. Wherever our ambivalence originates, Scripture provides a healing corrective. The God who created us so values our tears that he counts and collects them (Psalm 56:8). One day, he will wipe them gently away, because on that day there will be no more reason to cry (Revelation 21:4).

Throughout Scripture, we discover a God who hears and responds to the tears of the heartbroken. God hears Hannah's tears and gives her a son (1 Samuel 1:1–19); God hears

Hezekiah's tears and restores his health (Isaiah 38:2–5). David notes that God is counting and collecting his tears (Psalm 56:8). To those who have taught us to despise or fear our tears, we can only point to our tear-counting God, who saves them up until the day he will eradicate their source forever.

Because God cares for our tears, he sent his Son to this earth to grieve alongside us. When Jesus witnesses Mary's tears over her brother Lazarus' death, he weeps with his tear-dropping friends. Not long after this, Jesus will grieve again. In the Garden of Gethsemane, as he faces his impending separation from God, his agony causes him to sweat blood (Luke 22:44). Not tears from his eyes but blood from his body. Our tear-wiping Father sent his blood-sweating Son to suffer with and for us.

The same God who sent his tear-weeping Son for us will one day wipe away all of our tears, not because he doesn't want us to cry, but because there will be no more sin or sorrow. Imagine a good earthly father kneeling next to his wailing toddler, gently wiping the tears from his daughter's eyes, assuring her, "It's all okay now. Your dad is here. Nothing bad can hurt you again. The monsters are all slayed; the boo-boos are all healed." Such is the heart of our tear-wiping Father toward us.

Dear friends, you need not dry your eyes yet. But know that one day, you will be forever with your Father, and your Father will be forever with you. In that day, all the tears that he has collected will be redeemed, and there will be no more reason to weep.

Compassionate Father,

What good news that you cherish our tears. Thank you for sending your Son to weep with us. We look forward to the day when you will wipe all tears from our eyes as you restore all broken things. AMEN.

FURTHER ENCOURAGEMENT

- Read Psalm 56:8; Revelation 21:4; 1 Samuel 1:1–19; Isaiah 38:2–5.

- Listen to "Is He Worthy" by Andrew Peterson.

FOR REFLECTION

Have you ever felt you should not cry over the brokenness you are experiencing? How does it encourage you to know that God cares for your tears and will one day wipe them away?

NOTES

51

Getting Un-Stuck

*Come and see a man who told me everything
I ever did! Could he possibly be the Messiah?*
JOHN 4:29, NLT

RECOVERY CAN MAKE us feel stuck — stuck in isolation, stuck in guilt (whether legitimate or false), stuck in uncertainty, stuck in joylessness. The Samaritan woman of John 4 knew something about being stuck. She was stuck in a disastrous cycle of loving and losing men. Into this mucky rut, Jesus pursues her and pursues us, freeing us to do what we were made to do — to enjoy and glorify God.

The lonely Samaritan woman went daily at high noon to draw water, seeking to fill her thirst. She expected to be alone then, to escape the harsh glares of her disapproving community. Imagine her astonishment when a Jewish man crossed the cultural and racial divide to speak to her — a woman, a Samaritan. Imagine her astonishment when this Jewish teacher seemed to know "everything" about her, that the man she was currently living with was not her husband. Imagine her astonishment when this Jewish teacher didn't splash condemnation on her but instead poured out the truth and hope her thirsty heart craved (John 4:9–26).

Jesus did not come to condemn the Samaritan woman, nor did he come to condemn us; he came to expose our need for a Savior. He came to her and to us to restore us to community, to cover our shame, to fill our thirst. Jesus was on a mission from the Father, seeking out people who would "worship in spirit and in truth" (John 4:24 NLT), people who would enjoy and glorify God.

When the Samaritan woman reckoned with the truth about her condition and realized Jesus was the Messiah, she was instantly, radically changed. She dropped her water jar and headed to town, back to the very same people she had previously avoided, to share the good news: "Come, see a man who told me everything I ever did. Could this be the Messiah?" (John 4:29 NLT). She was un-stuck. She moved freely and joyously, running un-self-consciously. She must hurry to tell others, because the news she had was so great to give.

The Samaritan woman's radical transformation highlights Jesus' mercy to us when we are stuck in the ruts of recovery. Jesus seeks us in our hiding to draw us into community with the triune God and with fellow believers. He seeks us in our joylessness to remind us of our joy in him. He seeks us in our thirst to supply the living water that frees us to worship the Father in spirit and in truth.

When we seek out the Jesus who has already sought us out, we will be restored as worshippers of the Father. We will be unstuck, freed to move far beyond recovery. We will run with the Samaritan woman, moving out into the world to tell others about the Messiah who came to save us from our sins. We will enjoy and glorify God.

PRAYER

Jesus,

In this season, when we feel so stuck, we cry out to you. Free our hearts, souls, minds, and spirits so that we might tell others the good news about you. In your saving name. AMEN.

FURTHER ENCOURAGEMENT

- Read John 4:1–42.

- Listen to "The Love of God" by Sara Groves.

FOR REFLECTION

In what ways do you feel stuck right now? Ask Jesus to free you to see God's might and mercy in this area.

NOTES

52

New Creation

*Therefore, if anyone is in Christ, he
is a new creation. The old has passed
away; behold, the new has come.*
2 CORINTHIANS 5:17, ESV

POINTING TO THE mottled, roughened area on the MRI, my orthopedic surgeon explained that my hip joint was not supposed to look that way. Years of wear and tear had chewed up the cartilage and caused bone spurs to form, distorting its ability to function as it was created to do. The slick new synthetic ball and socket he planned to give me would glide smoothly through its range of motion, not catching or pinching or causing pain as my current one does.

My hip surgeon has something of a superpower — the ability to give me a new hip. But his power pales in comparison to the supernatural surgery performed by God through Christ. Our Creator actually takes our mottled, roughened, sinful selves, and remakes them, transforming them into new, righteous, whole selves. Whether it is our hips, our homes, or our households that have been wrecked by crisis, our new creation status offers profound hope.

How does God work this remarkable transformation in us? The process is somewhat like hip replacement, and yet far, far better. My orthopedic surgeon will place a new hip joint in me, using sutures to hold it all together. Eventually, the synthetic implant will grow into the old bone that remains, and they will be connected, working as one. Our Divine Surgeon places something far better in us—Christ's righteousness, and by his Spirit knits our new selves together. As God continues growing us up into Christ, our old self gives way to a new self. Day by day, year by year, God works through his Spirit to restore the image that was marred in the fall.

Just as my new hip will function more like the old one was designed to do, our new creation selves will recover their original God-fashioned purpose: to bear his fruit and multiply his glory. God sends us to the broken bodies, broken cities, and broken families we inhabit as "ambassadors of good news" and "ministers of reconciliation" (2 Corinthians 5:18–20). Not only do we have a story to tell; we are a living story that reveals the hope of the gospel to a hurting world. Not only can we offer reconciliation to others, we are living images of reconciliation, because we who were once enemies of God are now reconciled to him. As God's new creation, we become part of his restoration project.

And there is even better news! Unlike my new hip, which will one day wear out, our new creation selves will continue to be made new until the day when Christ returns to finish "making all things new" (Revelation 21:5). We do indeed have great cause for hope—in Christ, we are being formed and fashioned into new creations who look remarkably like the great builder and architect.

Creator God,

We thank you for taking our broken selves and remaking them into a marvelous new creation. Help us in this season to share the good news of your re-creation work with others and to bring your message of peace to a world that is desperately divided. In Christ's restoring name we pray. AMEN.

FURTHER ENCOURAGEMENT

- Read 2 Corinthians 5:16–21.

- Listen to "All Things New" by Steven Curtis Chapman.

FOR REFLECTION

In what way does seeing yourself as a new creation encourage you in your current story?

NOTES

53

Rejoicing in Reunion

*Let us rejoice and exult and give him the
glory, for the marriage of the Lamb has
come, and his Bride has made herself ready.*
REVELATION 19:7, ESV

THE CRASH OF divorce sends micro-fractures through a family system, leaving a limp not only in the once-married couple but also in their children, extended family, and friends. The social distancing of the global pandemic crisis has left people to grieve alone when loved ones were lost. Throughout history, the dividing walls of racism and tribalism have split God's family into false factions. Crisis often divides those who were meant to be joined together. There is good news, though—believers who have been separated by crisis will one day be reconciled and reunited to God and to one another. That day will be marked by the finest wedding ever planned.

The split of crisis can be traced back to the fall. In their rebellious act of eating the fruit forbidden by God, Adam and Eve became the first adulterers—they chose loyalty to Satan and their own desires over faithfulness to the God who had created them and abundantly blessed them. When their eyes were opened to their nakedness, they immediately sought to hide, attempting to cover themselves with faulty fig leaf garments, thus creating the first separation between male and female. Then, when they heard the Lord walking in the garden, they attempted to hide from their Creator (Genesis 3:8). Sin separates; sin divides; sin fragments our very being, limiting our capacity to enjoy God and to enjoy one another.

The good news of the gospel is that Jesus came to reunite what was divided in the fall: "But now in Christ Jesus, you who once were far off have been brought near by the blood of Christ" (Ephesians 2:13). Christ, who is our peace, reconciled not only the Jews and the Gentiles, but all who would trust in him, to God and to one another (Ephesians 2:14–18). Christ unites us to himself, making us "one new humanity," building us "together into a dwelling place for God by the Spirit" (Ephesians 2:15–19 NIV).

Even though we will wrestle with the split of sin and the fracture of the fall until the day Christ returns, we can trust that Christ is preparing us, his church, as his bride. Christ nourished and cherished his church, giving himself up for her that she might be sanctified. Daily, Christ's church grows more undivided in thought, word, and deed; she grows more in unadulterated delight in loving God and loving others (Ephesians 5:25–27). One day, Christ will present us to himself as a resplendent bride (Ephesians 5:27).

Today, if you feel divided by crisis, divided from God or from others, take heart. The day is coming when you will join the company of saints in a wildly wonderful wedding march. As Christ's lovely and holy bride, you, and all of the Church, will be reunited with your heavenly Bridegroom, and you will dance and feast in eternal joy with God the Father, Son, and Spirit.

PRAYER

Lord,

You have reconciled us to yourself, and you have restored broken relationships. We rejoice in the hope of our final wedding day, when we will be reunited with you forever. In Jesus' loving name. AMEN.

FURTHER ENCOURAGEMENT

- Read Ephesians 2:11–22; Revelation 19:6–9.

- Listen to "Blessed Be the Tie" by Sara Groves.

FOR REFLECTION

How does the reconciling work of Christ give you hope for any division crisis has caused in your life?

NOTES

54

No Evil Shall Be Allowed to Befall You

No evil shall be allowed to befall you,
no plague come near your tent.
PSALM 91:10, ESV

WHEN WE HAVE suffered the severe strikes of crisis—after the tornado has swept entire homes off their foundations or a global pandemic has stolen the lives of loved ones, the promises of Psalm 91 can seem false, even mocking. What are we to make of them? As Derek Kidner points out, we should not take the promises of Psalm 91 as a "charm against adversity," but rather an assurance that "nothing can touch God's servant but by God's leave."[27]

The Psalmist, whether David, Moses, or another, has previously experienced God as a safe shelter, as a refuge in storms (Psalm 91:1–2). David saw the Lord strike down the evil giant Goliath; Moses saw the Lord part the Red Sea when the evil Egyptians were breathing down the Israelites' necks. The Psalmist has known deliverance from deceit, deathly plagues, and deadly enemies (Psalm 91:1–3).

And yet, the Psalmist, like many of us, has also experienced severe betrayal—David was constantly fleeing from

Saul's attacks; Moses descended the mountain to find his own brother leading the people of God to worship a golden calf. This Psalmist, whoever he is, is not naïve about the Lord's protection. Indeed, terrors may come at night (Psalm 91:5), but we need not fear them because the Lord faithfully protects us from the worst evil—the destruction of our soul (Psalm 91:10).

We far too easily forget that a battle rages beyond the realm of this earth we inhabit. The Psalmist calls us to recognize the warfare of the spiritual realm. Like Elijah before us, we must envisage the massive battalions of angels God has set in place to shield us from the worst dangers, from dangers we never even knew about. We must look for God's powerful and otherworldly protection: God is "commanding his angels concerning you, to guard you in all your ways" (Psalm 91:11).

As we remember the battle in the spiritual realm, we recall that God rules over all evil, and that the day will come when the evil serpent will finally be trampled underfoot (Genesis 3:15; Psalm 91:13). Even though God may allow us to suffer physically, mentally, or emotionally on this earth, he will never allow evil to affect the salvation and final restoration of those who belong to him: "Because he holds fast to me in love, I will deliver him…" (Psalm 91:13).

Ultimately, because Jesus suffered for us, we will never suffer alone, and one day we will be "satisfied" with "long life" — forever delivered from the death snares of this world (Psalm 91:16). Dear friends, let us cling to the crucified as we look to that day of full restoration, when evil will never again befall us.

PRAYER

Lord, our Powerful Protector,

Help us grasp hold of you and hang on tight through all the snares and struggles of this life. May we see your powerful protection even in the severest suffering. Thank you for answering us when we call, for being with us in trouble. In Jesus' name. AMEN.

FURTHER ENCOURAGEMENT

- Read Psalm 91.

- Listen to "I Know Who Holds Tomorrow" by Alison Krauss.

FOR REFLECTION

How does it encourage you to know that the Lord has power over all evil?

NOTES

55

Walking Lessons

If we live in the Spirit, let us
also walk in the Spirit.
GALATIANS 5:25, NKJV

DROPPING MY SECOND crutch, I lurched around the kitchen like a drunken Frankenstein, trying to find my equilibrium. Despite being the proud owner of a new hip, I found myself walking less like the bionic woman and more like a wobbly toddler. The doctor had forewarned me that I would need to learn to walk again: "We changed all of the mechanics of your hip. Many of your muscles were impinged by the joint, so they haven't been working properly. With lots of physical therapy and plenty of practice, your new hip will function perfectly."

Just as my old hip's dysfunction caused me to walk improperly, the brokenness of crisis can lead us to develop sinful habits: we may decide to take matters into our own hands instead of trusting God, or we may become bitter and angry, blaming God and others. The hope for recovery comes from the new restoration story God is writing in us. Learning to walk in this new story happens as we rely on the work of the Spirit and practice new ways of living in the Spirit's power.

As we rely on the work of the Spirit, we learn to walk in our restoration story. Just as I rely on my physical therapist to break up scar tissue with a tool that looks suspiciously like a knife (albeit a butter knife), we rely on the Spirit, who labors in us to break up the "works of the flesh": envy and anger, idolatry and enmity, drunkenness and dissensions, just to name a few (Galatians 5:19–21). As we trust in the Spirit's sufficiency, our ultimate victory over sin is ensured, and we are gradually transformed to live in our new story.

Second, as we practice living in the Spirit's power, we learn how to walk in our new story. To learn to walk with my new hip, I need to do ten different exercises every day: three sets of fifteen reps. As we learn to walk in the Spirit, we must draw on his power to exercise our spiritual muscles: three sets of love, joy, peace, and patience; five sets of kindness, goodness, faithfulness, gentleness, and self-control. The good news is, the Spirit is working in us every day, all of the time, to enable us to walk in these healthy ways.

One day soon, I will no longer lurch around my kitchen like a drunken Frankenstein. And one day "soon," we will all dance elegantly as we are reunited with our bridegroom, Jesus. In that day, we will live freely, fully, and forever in the restoration story God has written in us.

PRAYER

Holy Spirit,

You are sufficient to defeat all of the sin and break up all of the scars which prevent us from walking freely in our restoration story. Continue your powerful work in us, and enable us to bear your fruit. AMEN

FURTHER ENCOURAGEMENT

- Read Galatians 5:1–25.

- Listen to "O For a Closer Walk with God" by Keith and Kristyn Getty.

FOR REFLECTION

In what ways are you learning to walk again in your recovery? How might you need to submit to the Spirit? How do you see the Spirit enabling you to walk and live in new ways?

NOTES

56

A New Normal

We rejoice in our sufferings, knowing
that suffering produces endurance,
and endurance produces character,
and character produces hope.
ROMANS 5:3–4, ESV

WE ALL KNOW people who have emerged from crisis with an exoskeleton of bitterness and anger wrapped around their hearts. Suffering changes our normal, sometimes for worse, sometimes for better. The gospel offers profound hope that we can inhabit a new, and even better normal, as God works his restoration hope into us. Romans 5:3–5 and 1 Peter 1:3–9 give us a glimpse into this better new normal: a life characterized by maturity grown through suffering.

Some psychologists describe "post-traumatic growth" that can follow trauma and suffering. Dr. Jamie Aten, author of *A Walking Disaster: What Surviving Katrina and Cancer Taught Me about Faith and Resilience*, describes the resilience he gained as "spiritual fortitude." He explains that this spiritual fortitude "helps people withstand adversity—especially when there is no clear end in sight—as they metabolize and lean into suffering."[28] Dr. Aten and other psychologists echo Paul and Peter, who both claim that suffering can mature us—beyond recovery, our new and better normal will include extraordinary endurance, proven character, confident hope, strengthened faith, extravagant love, and inexpressible joy. Let's consider how suffering leads to growth:

Extraordinary endurance (Romans 5:3): Fixing your eyes on Jesus, the "founder and perfecter" of your faith, who endured the cross for you, you keep walking forward, one new mercy at a time (Hebrews 12:2).

Proven character (Romans 5:4): You are growing "mature and complete" (James 1:4), becoming a person people trust as a wise and compassionate, tender and strong comforter. You don't toss out spiritual Band-Aids; you sit with those who suffer, listen carefully, and give wise counsel as the moment arises.

Confident hope (Romans 5:4–5): You are leaning into the future hope which "does not disappoint," the certain expectation that Jesus Christ is returning to restore and renew all shattered shalom.

Strengthened faith (1 Peter 1:7): Your faith, like gold being purified by a jeweler's fire, is strengthened and refined by trials. You have endured the agony of losing your home, your health, your spouse, or your job; when news of a pandemic arrives, your tested faith assures you that God will provide everything you need day by day.

Extravagant love (1 Peter 1:8): Your vision of the suffering Christ has been clarified and sharpened by your own suffering. You love Christ even more now than you did before, and you move into the world with that sacrificial love.

Inexpressible joy (1 Peter 1:8): You possess a joy that seems improbable given the circumstances of your life or the circumstances of this world. It is a joy based on the confident hope that God is at work even now restoring this broken world and your broken heart.

Dear friends, even in the midst of profound sorrow and loss, remember that you will one day move beyond recovery. In that day of the eternal new normal, you will know restoration hope that never fades.

PRAYER

Lord,

I confess, my current normal feels like it's killing me. May this suffering transform me, strengthening my endurance, my character, my faith, my hope, my love, and my joy. I long for the day when I will be with you, and I will be like you. In Jesus' name. AMEN.

FURTHER ENCOURAGEMENT

- Read 1 Peter 1:3–9.

- Listen to "We've Got This Hope" by Ellie Holcomb.

FOR REFLECTION

Can you see any glimpses of the new, better normal, God is writing into your story?

57

Seeking a Heavenly Homeland

For he was looking forward to the
city that has foundations, whose
designer and builder was God.
HEBREWS 11:10, ESV

OUR CITY WAS a wreck for months, really years, after the category four hurricane, Ivan, struck. The garish bright blue of vinyl tarps covered three out of four rooftops. Piles of debris spilled off curbs into streets. The buzz of chainsaws pierced the air. When we are living in a landscape of loss, we need the eyes of faith to look forward to the city with foundations, to envision our final destination, our "heavenly homeland" (Hebrews 11:14 NLT).

The author of Hebrews writes to a persecuted people, urging them to endure, telling them that they *will* endure by faith in Christ, their perfect Savior. This faith is defined as "the assurance of things hoped for, the conviction of things not seen" (Hebrews 11:1). Faith gives us the eyes to see this world and the next as God sees it. Hebrews 11 recounts the faith of many people, including Abraham, who viewed the world through this lens.

Abraham left his homeland of Haran, "not knowing where he was going" (Hebrews 11:8). God had promised him that he would be the father of many nations, and yet, he waited twenty-five long years for the birth of Isaac. Abraham reached the promised land, but he lived as a foreigner there, never possessing it as his own (Hebrews 11:9). Abraham was counted as one who saw God's promises and "greeted them from afar" (Hebrews 11:13). A stranger and exile on earth, Abraham shows us how to live in unfamiliar territory, always seeking the heavenly city that awaits us.

Unlike Abraham, we have received God's most precious promise in *our* lifetime—promised redemption in Jesus Christ. Like Abraham, we still look forward to the day when we will occupy our heavenly homeland. We have far more evidence for our hope than Abraham did. We have the memory of Christ, our King, defeating death by his resurrection. We have the Holy Spirit to give us eyes to see the future glory God has promised us. We have the firm reminder of Scripture that the devastation we witness today will one day pass away (1 Corinthians 7:31).

Dear friends, when you feel overwhelmed by the broken world you see all around you, put on the eyes of faith to envision the real city you will one day inhabit: "the holy city Jerusalem coming down out of heaven from God" (Revelation 21:10). Here, in this city, God's glory shines and sparkles like a crown bejeweled with sapphire and diamonds and emeralds and gold. Here, in this city, is a river gushing with life, a tree with leaves for the "healing of the nations" (Revelation 22:2). One day, you, and all who trust in Christ will dwell in this city looking fully in the face of its Holy Architect.

PRAYER

Dear Lord,

Give us the vision of faith to see beyond this ruined and ravaged world. Keep our eyes focused on the city you have designed and built for us, where you will restore all broken things. In Jesus' faithful name. AMEN.

FURTHER ENCOURAGEMENT

- Read Hebrews 11.

- Listen to "I Can Only Imagine" by Mercy Me.

FOR REFLECTION

What ruin and loss do you see in the world around you? Ask God to give you eyes to see what he is doing to prepare a better place for you.

NOTES

58

Beyond a Fixer-Upper

For behold, I create new heavens and a
new earth, and the former things shall
not be remembered or come to mind.
ISAIAH 65:17, ESV

OUR SON REQUIRED IV antibiotics four times a day for a wound infection he suffered after his second brain surgery. My father was spiraling down rapidly as prostate cancer did its ravaging work. Then we discovered that a wall of our home had been eaten by termites. Not only our wall, but our entire lives direly needed "fixing up." The good news of the gospel is that God is using even such seasons of crisis as part of his massive restoration project, a project that will fully and forever redeem our brokenness.

If you've ever seen a home restoration project show on TV, you know that the goal is not to return the house to its original condition; it's to use the "good bones" of the old creation and vastly improve upon it. Chip and Joanna Gaines replace shag carpets with heart pine, formica countertops with gleaming quartz, and beige drywall with shining shiplap. By the end of sixty minutes, the old ranch house looks like a palace.

In the same way, God does not replace the old creation; he restores it. He transforms broken things, making them new. As Pastor Scotty Smith says, God does not "make all new things, but all things new."

Isaiah 65:17-25 describes some of the transformations that will take place in God's restoration project, the full restoration of shalom:

Instead of "troubles, chaos, and pain," there will be joy, anticipation, and delight (Isaiah 65:17 MSG).

Instead of weeping in affliction and screaming in pain, there will be rejoicing and gladness (Isaiah 65:19).

Instead of babies dying when they are young or even before they have a chance to be born, there will be men and women living forever (Isaiah 65:20).

Instead of homes being destroyed by termites or tornados, there will be a permanent home with God. (Isaiah 65:22).

Instead of job frustration or joblessness, there will be fruitful, earth-filling work (Isaiah 65:23).

Instead of children's lives heading in disastrous directions, there will be the multicultural, multigenerational family of God (Isaiah 65:23).

Instead of broken communication with God, there will be his delight eternally sung over us (Isaiah 65:24).

Instead of men abusing women or vice-versa, or one race or tribe abusing another; there will be perfect peace and reconciliation (Isaiah 65:25).

Our Creator God is in the midst of a marvelous restoration project, and we are part of it. Whatever pain or trouble assaults us today, we are living toward the day when there will be no more affliction or destruction (Isaiah 65:25).

PRAYER

Oh Lord,

Thank you for the good news that in Christ you are making all things new, and that one day, your restoration project will be completed. We so long for that day. In Jesus' name. AMEN.

FURTHER ENCOURAGEMENT

- Read Isaiah 65:17–25.

- Listen to "We Will Feast in the House of Zion" by Sandra McCracken.

FOR REFLECTION

Review the list of things that will be "forgotten" and things that will be enjoyed in the new heavens and the new earth. Which do you look forward to the most?

NOTES

59

When the Lord Restored Our Fortunes

When the Lord restored the fortunes of
Zion, we were like those who dream.
PSALM 126:1, ESV

WE JOKED AND we jostled. We swam with a dolphin and snor-keled with a turtle. We danced the macarena. Some of us sang karaoke. Our younger son, now twenty-four, flew down the "daredevil" waterslide with his siblings and in-laws, laughing with glee. It did, indeed, seem like a dream. Memories of the sorrowful season two years before had faded. Gone was the tension, the pain, the fear we had all known during the year our younger son underwent four brain surgeries. Now we were cruising through paradise, our mouths filled with laughter.

It might be today. It might be tomorrow. It might be next year. It might take longer. But one day, in the new heavens and the new earth, we will all have our mouths filled with laughter and our tongues wagging with shouts of joy. The Lord has already returned us to himself through the death and resurrec-tion of Jesus Christ, but one day, he will finish restoring our fortunes. In that day, he will free us forever from captivity to sin; he will restore us fully to himself. This restoration will be marked by many blessings, including:

Reunion: In that day, the loneliness of exile, the agony of betrayal, the loss of loved ones, will evaporate like ground fog giving way on a sunny day. The Lord will return us — to unbroken communion with himself, to undivided community with others. We will be joined together like loyal football fans, except we will sing out the praises of our good God and shout out our gratitude for our gracious Redeemer.

Freedom from sin: In that day, we will no longer be imprisoned by our own sin, nor held captive by the brokenness of the fallen world. The Lord will return us to the freedom of living and loving unhampered by selfishness. The Lord will restore our glorious purpose, enabling us to enjoy him and make his name great.

Fruitfulness and joy: In that day, we will see that our tears shed in crisis did not fall lifeless on the ground. Indeed, the Lord took those tears and sowed them in his rich soil of mercy. In that day, the fruit of our tears will poke life out of the dirt of this fallen world, emerging as bright green sprouts, waving in the wind in a joyful dance.

It might seem like a dream. It might seem too good to be true. We will not believe our good "fortune." We will be with God! We will swim with dolphins and turtles. But it won't be a dream. It will be real. In that day, we will say with the nations, "The Lord has done great things for us; we are glad" (Psalm 126:3). Let's lean toward that day, dear friends. It is coming soon.

PRAYER

Lord,

Thank you for growing the fruit of your glory out of the tears we have wept. Thank you for dream-like days, days filled with laughter and joy. We look forward to the day when the dream-like days will last forever, because we will be with you. Until that day comes, keep our eyes fixed on the horizon. In Jesus' name. AMEN.

FURTHER ENCOURAGEMENT

- Read Psalm 126.

- Listen to "Come Light Our Hearts" by Sandra McCracken.

FOR REFLECTION

Write about a time that your sorrow gave way to joy. Or, if you can't think of one, tell what it would be like if your sorrow gave way to joy. What joy do you see the Lord restoring?

NOTES

60

Full and Forever Healing

The leaves of the tree were for
the healing of the nations.
REVELATION 22:2, ESV

WE BEGAN IN the recovery room, we end in the fully restored new heavens and new earth. Here, as Pastor Scotty Smith puts it, "the healing of the nations will come to completion. The substantive healing we can know in this life will give way to the fullness of his peace in eternity."[29] What will life be like here, beyond recovery?

There will no longer be "anything accursed" (Revelation 22:3). No more sea—that is, chaos and confusion (Revelation 21:1). (Gulf coast inhabitants feel sure our sugar sands and teal seas will abound in the new heavens and new earth.) No more sin or sinners, for only those washed clean by the blood of Christ are allowed to enter this wonderful city (Revelation 22:14–15). No more suffering or sorrow, for the Lord himself has put an end to all mourning and crying and pain and wiped all tears away (Revelation 21:4). Healing is complete; harmony reigns.

In this shimmering city-garden, all of creation will be rejoined in joy, reunited with God and reunited with one another, fully healed by the leaves of the tree of life. There will be neither night nor light from lamps or sun, for the light of the glorious Lord will flood us with his bright delight (Revelation 22:5). In that day, we will, indeed, be like him, "for we will see him as he really is" (1 John 3:2 NLT).

Our thirst for right-ness and righteousness will be forever quenched as we drink deeply from the river of the water of life: his "inexhaustible grace."[30] As his perfected and glorified Bride, we will invite others to drink of this grace with us, crying, "Let the one who is thirsty come; let the one who desires take the water of life without price" (Revelation 22:17).

Finally, we will fulfill our exquisite design of enjoying God and worshiping him forever. As we feast with God, we will hear stories of how all along he was working crises out for our good and for his glory. We will clap our hands and dance for joy as we fully know his kind and kingly rule. As we move into this full knowledge of our King and Bridegroom, we will reign forever with him, executing his original mission for us: "Be fruitful and multiply. Fill the earth and govern it" (Genesis 1:28 NLT). And, because all of creation has been liberated from its bondage to sin and death, we will be fruitful, and we will multiply—God's glory through all the earth.

Oh, friends, can you see it? Can you hear the Bridegroom calling to you? Three times in the final chapter of the Bible, he says, "Surely, I am coming soon" (Revelation 22:7, 12, 20). Will you join with the voice of all the saints in response, "Come, Lord Jesus!" (Revelation 22:20)? Fret not, for the day of restoration will soon arrive, bringing to an end our season in recovery.

PRAYER

Father God,

As we look forward to the day when the grace of the Lord Jesus will be with us forever, the day when you will return and restore all broken things, we rejoice and we respond,

"Come, Lord Jesus." AMEN.

FURTHER ENCOURAGEMENT

- Read Revelation 21 and 22.
- Listen to "I Am Making All Things New" by Wendell Kimbrough.

FOR REFLECTION

In what ways does envisioning what life will be like in the fully restored new heavens and new earth give you hope in your current season?

NOTES

Acknowledgments

To walk the road from recovery to restoration is to know your complete dependence on others. I am indebted to many, including…

My Lord and Savior Jesus Christ.

My husband, Kirby Loftin Turnage III, faithful companion and generous caregiver through many seasons of recovery.

Our children and your spouses—it is a profound joy to watch your adult children walk through sorrow and joy with strong faith, sincere hope, and genuine love. And how sweet to enjoy so much time together this year, even if it was because of a global pandemic:

> Robert Reynolds Turnage
> Mary Elizabeth and Caleb Blake
> Jackie and Matt Roelofs
> Kirby and Amy Anne Turnage

My mother, Jackie Reynolds, my faithful cheerleader, for your daily encouragement, and for your love of reading which has nurtured my love of the written word.

My in-laws, Kirby and Joy Turnage, for your loving support.

Pastoral friends who consistently turn me toward my true restoration hope: Scotty and Darlene Smith, Hope Parker, Cheryl Simcox, Christie Tilley, Mary Baker, and Joel and Kate Treick.

The many people who prayed for this work, read early chapters, and offered insight and encouragement along the way, especially:

Susan Calderazzo, Cindy Jank, Kelly Markham, Suzy Marshall, Meaghan May, and Peggy Orren.

The body of our local church: Pinewoods Presbyterian.

Editor Ed Eubanks: for your skill and grace in refining my words and thoughts. Any errors remaining are mine alone.

Cover Designer Erik M. Peterson: for engaging with the story and sharing it through your splendid artistic creation.

Typesetter and Interior Formatter/Designer Charity Walton of Good Shepherd Publications: for your excellent work and your cheerful spirit.

Last, but not least, my longtime care team: Ken Byrd, physical therapist, Zac Hastings, Ken's skilled and compassionate assistant. My orthopedic doctors, Eric Kujowski and Kurt Morrison, excellent physicians and kind caregivers. Your kind care has given me hope for recovery through the years.

Appendix

GOD HAS PROVIDED numerous creative ways to manage stress and heal from crisis. I pray you will enjoy these resources.

MUSIC

You can find a playlist of most of the songs mentioned in this book on YouTube at
https://www.youtube.com/playlist?list=PL7Ye1tLnHUSb-3Wxy08QINDgIX3zXTxJ72
and on Spotify at
https://open.spotify.com/playlist/6TTWKWAMUGOjRz-jf4hzzbt?si=4JGB2h7kTk-fGKn0e6Jvug.

RELAXATION ACTIVITIES

BREATHING

Breathing techniques have been shown to reduce anxiety and stress. Try one of these techniques from the University of Michigan Health Library:
https://www.uofmhealth.org/health-library/uz2255.

WALKING

Exercise has been shown to alleviate stress. Even several ten-minute walks around the house, especially outside, can benefit greatly. For more information, see Exercise for Stress and Anxiety:
https://adaa.org/living-with-anxiety/managing-anxiety/exercise-stress-and-anxiety#:~:text=Scientists%20have%20found%20that%20regular,to%20stimulate%20anti%2Danxiety%20effects.

PRAYER

In addition to the prayers in this book, Elizabeth provides daily gospel-centered prayers.

Instagram (@etstory): https://www.instagram.com/etstory/

Facebook (Elizabeth Reynolds Turnage, Author): https://www.facebook.com/ElizabethReynoldsTurnage/

ART

FREE COLORING PAGES

Karla Dornacher: https://www.karladornacher.com/freebies/

God's Fingerprints: https://godsfingerprints.co/blogs/blog/3-creative-ways-to-use-your-bible-coloring-pages

WATERCOLOR

Sarah Cray, Letsmakeart.com: Free watercolor tutorials and outlines.

JOURNALING

BIBLE AND ART JOURNALING

Sue Kemnitz: https://suekemnitz.com and book: Honoring the Spirit at amzn.to/2N8tIV1

Anita C. Haines: Trusting in God at amzn.to/2NAJRBV

Karla Dornacher: Everlasting Hope at amzn.to/2NAJVSb

GRATITUDE JOURNALS

Keeping a gratitude journal can be as simple as making a list of things you are thankful for. You can use the Notes App on your phone, or a small pocket-sized notebook. For more on this, check out the resources below as well as Elizabeth's free gratitude journal for subscribers: http://eepurl.com/b__teX (Select *From Recovery to Restoration* on signup).

30 GRATITUDE JOURNAL PROMPTS

http://textmyjournal.com/gratitude-journal-prompts/.

GRATITUDE AND PRAYER JOURNALS FOR PURCHASE

Shannon Roberts: *Prayer Journal for Women: 52 Week Scripture, Devotional & Guided Prayer Journal* at amzn.to/38Jsc2Z.

Ben Greenfield: *Christian Gratitude Journal* at amzn.to/2x-aRnZU: masculine gratitude journal and planner.

Notes

1   *Merriam-Webster.com Dictionary*, s.v. "crisis," https://www.merriam-webster.com/dictionary/crisis.

2   Ibid.

3   Cornelius Plantinga, *Not the Way It's Supposed to Be: A Breviary of Sin* (Grand Rapids: Eerdmans 1995), 9-10.

4   Joni Eareckson Tada, in *Beyond Suffering Bible* (Carol Stream, Il.: Tyndale House, 2016), 919.

5   Thomas Chisholm, "Great Is Thy Faithfulness" (Carol Stream, Il.: Hope Publishing, 1951), at Hymnal.net, https://www.hymnal.net/en/hymn/h/19.

6   Jill Carrattini, "Waiting for Light," RZIM.org, https://www.rzim.org/read/a-slice-of-infinity/waiting-for-light-4.

7   We should note that some symptoms of anxiety may need to be addressed by a physician or professional counselor.

8   Charles Spurgeon, "Prisoners of Hope," at SpurgeonGems.org, http://www.spurgeongems.org/sermon/chs2839.pdf.

9   Scotty Smith, "Living as Prisoners of Hope," Sermon, First Presbyterian Church, Ocean Springs, MS, April 19, 2019, at http://www.fpcosms.com/sermons/living-as-prisoners-of-hope/.

10 Charles Spurgeon, *THE VALLEY OF THE SHADOW OF DEATH NO. 1595*, SpurgeonGems.org, https://www.spurgeongems.org/vols25-27/chs1595.pdf, 3.

11 The Westminster Shorter Catechism Question #1, at ShorterCatechism.com, https://www.shortercatechism.com/resources/wsc/wsc_001.html.

12 (šāmar) in R. Laird Harris, Gleason L. Archer Jr., and Bruce K. Waltke, eds., *Theological Wordbook of the Old Testament* (Chicago: Moody Press, 1999), 939.

13 Dan Allender and Tremper Longman III, *Cry of the Soul* (Colorado Springs: NavPress, 1994), 155.

14 Ann Voskamp, *One Thousand Gifts: A Dare to Live Fully Right Where You Are* (Grand Rapids: Zondervan, 2011), 125.

15   R. Kent Hughes, *2 Corinthians: Power in Weakness* (Wheaton: Crossway, 2006), 99.

16   Ibid.

17   Abby Hutto, *God for Us: Discovering the Heart of the Father through the Life of the Son* (Phillipsburg, N.J.: P & R, 2019), 90.

18   Reverend Joel Treick, "Desperate Times, Desperate Measures," Sermon, Pinewoods Presbyterian Church, July 28, 2019, http://www.pinewoodschurch. org/resources/sermons/month/7-2019/.

19   *Dictionary of Biblical Imagery*, Tremper Longman III, Leland Ryken, and James C. Wilhoit, gen. eds. (Downer's Grove: InterVarsity, 1998), s.v. "sheep," 782.

20   Nathan Bierma, *Bringing Heaven Down to Earth: Connecting This Life to the Next* (Phillipsburg: P & R Publishing, 2005), 56.

21   Ibid, 56.

22   Joni Eareckson Tada, *A Place of Healing: Wrestling with the Mysteries of Suffering, Pain, and God's Sovereignty* (Colorado Springs: David C. Cook, 2010), 55-56.

23   Richard D. Phillips, *Hebrews* (Phillipsburg, NJ: P&R Publishing, 2006), 119–120.

24   Mary Beth Chapman, Ellen Vaughn, Steven Curtis Chapman, *Choosing to See: A Journey of Struggle and Hope* (Grand Rapids: Revell, 2010), 89.

25   John Stott, *The Message of 1 and 2 Thessalonians* (Downer's Grove: Intervarsity Press, 1991), 96.

26   Karen Swallow Prior, *On Reading Well: Finding the Good Life through Great Books* (Grand Rapids: Brazos, 2018), 192.

27   Derek Kidner, *Psalms 73-150* (London: Intervarsity Press, 1975), 365.

28   Jamie Aten, PhD, *A Walking Disaster: What Surviving Katrina and Cancer Taught Me about Faith and Resilience* (West Conshohocken, PA: Templeton Press, 2018), 187.

29   Scotty Smith, *Revelation: Hope in the Darkness* (Greensboro: New Growth Press, 2020), 135.

30   Philip Hughes, *The Book of the Revelation* (Grand Rapids: Eerdsman, 1990), 232, quoted in Smith, *Revelation: Hope in the Darkness*, 134.

Scripture Index

NEW TESTAMENT

Complete Song List

	Meditation	Song Title	Link
1.	Be of Good Cheer	"What a Friend"	https://youtu.be/B3JT1kuSTlY
2.	Landscape of Loss	"Mercy Leads"	https://youtu.be/BCpfTa2Ci7o
3.	Telling It Like It Is: Lament	"Come Lift Up Your Sorrows"	https://youtu.be/H3vwApmk-Z4
4.	His Mercies Are New	"Great Is Thy Faithfulness"	https://www.youtube.com/watch?v=2eQ1oal44wU
5.	Do Not Fear	"Abide with Me"	https://youtu.be/84YASWe3_2Q
6.	Revive My Soul	"Speak, O Lord"	https://youtu.be/qNCHZrwlo9c
7.	Waiting or Whining	"I Will Wait for You"	https://youtu.be/dwovhY8zNQM
8.	Darkness Overcome	"To the Dawn"	https://youtu.be/Jpiyd4iPkPc
9.	Scan-xiety, Triggers, and Aftershocks	"Be Still My Soul"	https://www.youtube.com/watch?v=mq59iE3MhXM
10.	Throwing Off Anxiety	"Be Not Dismayed"	https://youtu.be/CaDj00gU9w4
11.	Set Your Mind on Things Above	"Turn Your Eyes upon Jesus"	https://youtu.be/L57ox0iQU7A
12.	Unspoken	"Arise My Soul, Arise"	https://youtu.be/UuJ7-s3gN4k.
13.	Prisoners of Hope	"Jesus Shall Reign"	https://youtu.be/BE4DDD5whyk
14.	You Are with Me	"God Is My Shepherd"	https://www.youtube.com/watch?v=LtDXHgTi-5s
15.	Naked and Unashamed	"With Great Gentleness"	https://youtu.be/PTq01rO-_wc
16.	Never Forsaken	"You Are My King"	https://youtu.be/MA_cSFdUMqk

Meditation	Song Title	Link
17. A Safe Place	"This Is Our God"	https://youtu.be/z4Dd-BH4Lks
18. The Accuser	"Power in the Blood"	https://youtu.be/ncNSz13hyNM
19. Enjoying God	"Rejoice the Lord Is King"	https://youtu.be/ohOBYrdd-8o
20. All Your Needs	"I Need Thee Every Hour"	https://youtu.be/8tnEm4NXE58
21. Pray about Everything	"Sweet Hour of Prayer"	https://youtu.be/EwOPwAVDN7s
22. Surpassing Peace	"Find You Here"	https://youtu.be/94rRsRlYPrw
23. Call Me Bitter	"Fool's Gold"	https://youtu.be/RdBOQgYALyA
24. Courage for Crisis	"Lead On O King Eternal"	https://youtu.be/Jdi6vLGthrI
25. The Sleep of the Beloved	"Sleepless Night"	https://youtu.be/fJO1ng7lBTE
26. Waiting with Hope	"Spring Is Coming"	https://youtu.be/lCmMWO_XFXO
27. Give Thanks in All Circumstances	"10,000 Reasons"	https://youtu.be/2KaHr_5U9Cg
28. Joy Comes	"Joyful, Joyful, We Adore Thee"	https://youtu.be/ApUEbObOTLc
29. When You Despair of Life Itself	"God of All Comfort"	https://youtu.be/MW9gKuLpbTU
30. Christ's Power for Your Weakness	"How Firm a Foundation"	https://youtu.be/ILmDxqg-_Ck
31. Two Crucial Questions	"Who Is Like Our God"	https://youtu.be/2IOays2yZkc
32. Though He Slay Me	"Blessed Be Your Name"	https://youtu.be/tTpTQ4kBLxA
33. The Good News of Not Being Fine	"Kindness"	https://youtu.be/is86D_ueopM
34. Another Helper	"Holy Spirit, Living Breath of God"	https://youtu.be/kDYjn-YdnD4

Meditation	Song Title	Link
35. The God Who Is for You	"It Is Well with My Soul"	https://youtu.be/zY5o9mP22V0
36. Go into Peace	"Heal Us Emmanuel"	https://youtu.be/k8EA-EcBMMg
37. All We Like Sheep	"The King of Love My Shepherd Is"	https://www.youtube.com/watch?v=il1OeQfkVyI
38. Your Kingdom Come	"King of Love"	https://youtu.be/LOXvlp5Ob3A
39. Instead of Ashes	"There Will Be a Great Rejoicing"	https://www.youtube.com/watch?v=9kQOrjQDRu4
40. But God Intended It for Good	"Where No One Stands Alone"	https://youtu.be/djsiL-G88rY.
41. Quick Fixes and Faith Healings	"Blessings"	https://youtu.be/JKPeoPiK9XE
42. Scar Tissue	"Though You Slay Me"	https://youtu.be/qyUPz6_TciY
43. A Purpose for Your Pain	"May the Mind of Christ My Savior"	https://www.youtube.com/watch?v=2JkNwT6DGOs
44. Good News of Great Joy	"My Soul Magnifies the Lord"	https://youtu.be/HHzevDE3xhU
45. Surrender	"Be Born in Me"	https://youtu.be/QsXOP7aQeqQ.
46. The Rest of Restoration	"Good to Me"	https://youtu.be/bKosVfAEUPE
47. Grieving with Hope	"See"	https://youtu.be/BeeyJ8ajglw
48. I Believe Help My Unbelief	"Help My Unbelief"	https://youtu.be/d_KKZxwYTZ4
49. The Lord's Perfect Timing	"Oh God Our Help in Ages Past"	https://youtu.be/HTBV_mN3Ktg
50. Our Tear-Wiping Father	"Is He Worthy"	https://youtu.be/Olahc83Kvp4
51. Getting Unstuck	"The Love of God"	https://youtu.be/wRvrYONPPTk
52. New Creation	"All Things New"	https://youtu.be/FhpQN9JXNXA

Meditation	Song Title	Link
53. Rejoicing in Reunion	"Blessed Be the Tie"	https://www.youtube.com/watch?v=gcYFtihSg_8
54. No Evil Shall Be Allowed to Befall You	"I Know Who Holds Tomorrow"	https://youtu.be/B3rlzgXJBX0
55. Walking Lessons	"O For a Closer Walk with God"	https://youtu.be/e7PdQRbzKgU
56. A New Normal	"We've Got This Hope"	https://youtu.be/OnuC_zEugo0
57. Seeking a Heavenly Homeland	"I Can Only Imagine"	https://youtu.be/N_lrrq_opng
58. Beyond a Fixer-Upper	"We Will Feast in the House of Zion"	https://youtu.be/d1ylQhnRx-A.
59. When the Lord Restored Our Fortunes	"Come Light Our Hearts"	https://youtu.be/tV_KPx6QRos
60. Full and Forever Healing	"I Am Making All Things New"	https://youtu.be/Tn8hQy54R9Y

ENJOYED THIS BOOK? Reading a borrowed copy, or want to gift a friend? Please consider taking the next step:

Purchase your own copy at favorite booksellers, or visit www.elizabethturnage.com/FromRecoverytoRestoration.

CONSIDER SHARING THIS BOOK WITH OTHERS:

Write a book review on Amazon, Goodreads, or your favorite platform. This helps others find the book and enjoy it too.

Share or mention on your social media platforms. Use the hashtag #FromRecoverytoRestoration

WANT MORE GOOD GOSPEL-CENTERED RESOURCES?

Get free journaling prompts, planners, story starters, prayer cards, and more. Sign up at http://eepurl.com/b__teX.

CONNECT WITH THE AUTHOR:

Elizabeth Reynolds Turnage, author, gospel coach, and Bible teacher, is the founder of Living Story ministries (www.elizabethturnage.com). She is passionate about helping people learn, live, and love in God's story of grace. Elizabeth is the author of *The Waiting Room: 60 Meditations for Finding Peace & Hope in a Health Crisis* as well as three Bible studies published by P&R Publishing. Elizabeth has been married to Kip Turnage for 38 years, and they enjoy feasting and telling good stories with their four adult children and three children-in-law. They are also the ridiculously proud "parents" of a beloved goldendoodle, Rosie.

I'd love to hear from you. You can reach me in the following ways:

https://www.elizabethturnage.com

https://www.facebook.com/ElizabethReynoldsTurnage/

https://www.instagram.com/etstory/

https://www.youtube.com/channel/
UCJd3himKaNSHaHpo21DcFlw

https://www.linkedin.com/in/elizabethturnage/

https://twitter.com/elizturnage

https://www.pinterest.com/elizabeth_turn/the-waiting-room/

Other books by
Elizabeth Reynolds Turnage

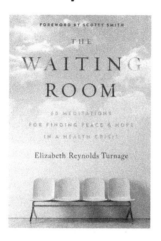

- *The Waiting Room: 60 Meditations for Finding Peace & Hope in a Health Crisis:* Living Story, 2019

- *Learning in God's Story of Grace:* P & R, 2010

- *Living in God's Story of Grace:* P & R, 2011

- *Loving in God's Story of Grace:* P & R, 2014